CHAPTER 12

TESTIMONIALS

Our team has always appreciated your professional expertise in helping us help our clients to connect the most effective strategies and tools with their heartfelt support of what matters to them.

Patrick J Green, Partner,
Davis Wright Tremaine, LLP

Arlene Siegel Cogen is a true professional. Her infectious personality and deep knowledge of charitable gift planning make her an absolute pleasure to work with. Ever since I arrived in Portland eight years ago she has been a wonderful resource, advocate and friend.

Marc Blattner, CEO of Jewish Federation
of Greater Portland

I had the pleasure of working with Arlene for several years when she was with The Oregon Community Foundation, and she clearly "gets" the world of philanthropy.

Jeffrey C. Thede, Partner, Thede, Culpepper,
Moore, Monroe & Silliman, LLP

I have had the privilege of knowing Arlene for many years. I find her to be warm, compassionate, and fun, with a no nonsense personality. She is knowledgeable in her field of expertise and is a thoughtful, strategic thinker. It has been my pleasure to have her coach my colleagues as well as introduce her to my clients. I will look forward to working with Arlene throughout the years to come.

**Michelle Castano Garcia, Principal,
Northwest Investment Counselors**

I have known Arlene as a congregant and consultant for the past 4 years. As a campaign professional she has helped galvanize, energize and educate our core of solicitors. She is professional, kind and supportive.

**Eve Posen, Assistant Rabbi,
Congregation Neveh Shalom**

ABOUT THE AUTHOR

Arlene Cogen, CFP

Arlene Cogen is an experienced philanthropic leadership consultant who works closely with professional advisors, nonprofits, and their clients to foster deep relationships, engage the next generation, and make a lasting difference through leadership and philanthropy.

A Certified Financial Planner (CFP), Arlene spent over 20 years in the trust and investment world on the leadership teams of numerous major financial institutions. Desiring change and the opportunity to give back, Arlene acquired nonprofit development expertise and excellence by helping to guide the ninth largest community foundation in the country for almost a decade.

Arlene was the first nonprofit leader to hold a board position on the Portland Estate Planning Council. Arlene's other professional affiliations include the Financial Planning Association, National Speakers Association, Northwest Planned Giving Roundtable, and the Oregon Philanthropic Advisors Network.

When you work with Arlene, you get an expert perspective on giving derived from her broad experiences with individuals and businesses ranging from Wall Street to Main Street.

ArleneCogen.com
Arlene@ArleneCogen.com
503-957-8334

THANK YOU

When I walk into a sacred space, I say the Shehecheyanu. The Shehecheyanu blessing is said on special occasions and when thankful for new and unusual experiences. For me, writing this book was a sacred duty, and the completion was the ultimate special occasion.

בָּרוּךְ אַתָּה יְיָ אֱלֹהֵינוּ מֶלֶךְ הָעוֹלָם, שֶׁהֶחֱיָנוּ וְקִיְּמָנוּ וְהִגִּיעָנוּ לַזְּמַן הַזֶּה.

Baruch atah Adonai, Eloheinu Melech haolam, shehecheyanu, v'kiy'manu, v'higianu laz'man hazeh

Our praise to You, Eternal our God, Sovereign of all: for giving us life, sustaining us, and enabling us to reach this season.

If you found this book valuable, make an appointment with your advisors to discuss your legacy and begin your philanthropic journey.

Follow me on social Media.

LinkedIn: https://www.linkedin.com/in/arlenecogen/
Twitter: @ArleneCogen

Have FUN doing the most good.

Arlene

Arlene@arlenecogen.com
ArleneCogen.com

Give to Live chronicles a wonderful account of the author's journey to a deep appreciation and understanding of the concept and benefits of personal philanthropy. Throughout the book, the author identifies different vignettes identifying how charitable giving can accommodate the needs of those engaged in estate planning, and further identifies the importance of and self satisfaction derived from the concept of personal philanthropy. The book is an excellent read for those who are considering charitable giving as a component of their estate planning and for the advisers who assist them in developing an appropriate, responsible and fulfilling plan.

Stephen E. Kantor, Partner, Samuels Yoelin Kanter, LLP

"This book is truly a gift from Arlene-she shares her heart and passion for thoughtful philanthropy. Her experience makes "Give to Live" an invaluable resource for givers and the professional who work with them."

Carolyn W. Miller, Carolyn W. Miller, P.C.

"Arlene provides a practical primer on the basics of philanthropy as part of estate planning by presenting valuable information woven throughout inspirational stories. This book is valuable to anyone who wants a better understanding of their options in creating a personal legacy."

James K. Phelps, ACFRE, JKP Fundraising, LLC

"With Arlene's experience in financial and charitable planning, she's perfectly suited to advise donors and their families on effective philanthropy. *Give to Live* is a great study on how diverse charitable planning strategies can be applied to a donor's individual financial situation to help achieve the donor's particular philanthropic goals."

Jeffrey C. Thede, Partner, Thede, Culpepper, Moore, Monroe & Silliman, LLP

"This beautifully written book will inspire you with its words of wisdom. If you're looking for an excuse not to think about philanthropy and giving because it's just too complicated; your justification will vanish after reading this book. Well organized, thoughtful, with actionable and clear steps, you can find your way through the terms and concepts of giving. You'll become excited at the possibilities and ideas you discover in these pages, and leave a legacy that brings you peace of mind. The world of philanthropy has been waiting for this book, and because of its message, people who never knew it was possible will leave lasting gifts that will change the world."

Victoria Trabosh, CEC, Victoria Trabosh Executive Coach, LLC

"I appreciate the personal experiences that Arlene shares in this book. She has a way of making complex information relatable and understandable adding tremendous value to individuals and families alike. Her passion for helping people leave a legacy, a legacy they never dreamed possible is awe inspiring. Thank you for sharing your wisdom."

Michelle Castano Garcia, Principal, Northwest Investment Counselors

"As an estate planning lawyer in Portland, I have known Arlene Cogen as a trust officer, development officer at a community foundation, and charitable-planning consultant. She is a caring professional, and her book is a heartfelt and accessible overview of charitable giving."

Jonathan A. Levy, Attorney, Wyse Kadish, LLP

"This book is easy to read and understand, especially for someone who doesn't have knowledge of the financial world. It is an essential and valuable resource as you begin to figure out your estate planning and will. Using the information from this book my husband and I were able to dig deeper into the kind of giving we feel comfortable with and have the language to express that to our financial planner."

Rabbi Eve Posen, Assistant Rabbi, Congregation Neveh Shalom

"If you're thinking about some serious (for you) giving to support community services you care about, this book will give you lots of help in thinking about that in ways that make sense to you.

If you're not thinking about that, this book will give you some ideas about how you can enhance your life (and your family's) by giving during your lifetime and afterward.

Arlene Cogen's experience enables her to provide lots of examples of people like you and me who have found that we can give well to organizations which deliver the services we care about in ways that make us glad we're doing that. And she gives us lots of ways of lowering our net cost of giving."

Jim Meyer, Owner, Criterion Investment Company LLC

"This book is easy to read and understand. It breaks down the concepts of giving into understandable terms. It provides actionable steps and is a valuable resource as you begin to fold philanthropy into your overall planning."

Sharna Goldseker, Executive Director, 21/64

GIVE TO
LIVE

MAKE A CHARITABLE GIFT
YOU NEVER IMAGINED

GIVE TO LIVE

MAKE A CHARITABLE GIFT YOU NEVER IMAGINED

ARLENE COGEN, CFP®

Niche Pressworks

Indianapolis

For permission to reprint portions of this content or bulk purchases, contact Arlene Cogen at 503-957-8334 or Arlene@arlenecogen.com

Published by Niche Pressworks, Indianapolis, IN
http://NichePressworks.com

Printed in the United States of America

DEDICATION

To my parents, Ada and Abraham Siegel, of blessed memory

PREFACE

I began writing this book to help people understand the giving process. But, after many hours of writing, I realized it was about more than giving. It was about taking care of your family and making a difference. What I've written is a guide—one that explains how to make giving, or philanthropy, a meaningful and rewarding part of your life. Through the inspiring stories of people I've worked with, you will learn how family situations that sometimes appear to present insurmountable obstacles can be transformed and result in priceless gifts for both the donors and recipients. It's a win-win situation, and it all begins when you make a charitable donation you may never have imagined.

In the pages that follow, I offer a unique perspective on solving challenging family situations and overcoming obstacles by adding a charitable element to your financial plan. Through the creative use of philanthropy, this book helps envision solutions, such as engaging multiple generations in philanthropy to pass down values, life lessons and stories, and providing an income stream to a child who "failed to launch"—all while simultaneously aiding the world through benevolence.

Whether you are new to giving or simply keen to improve your understanding of financial planning and philanthropy, this is your book. It will free you from the haze of complicated jargon, break things down in understandable terms, and share ways to effectively and meaningfully include giving in your life. Additionally, this book will help you learn how to pick the best advisors to help with your financial planning and how to best engage with those advisors to obtain your philanthropic, financial, and family goals.

Enjoy the journey.

ACKNOWLEDGEMENTS

"You must do the thing you think you cannot do."

—Eleanor Roosevelt

Where shall I begin to acknowledge everyone who helped me create this book? I can go back to the first time I uttered the words, "I'm going to write a book." What a crazy idea for someone who hates writing. What was I thinking?!

I'll start with Mitch Cogen, my best friend, husband, and the love of my life. He has been supportive of me since the moment we met. He has also been my behind-the-scenes writer and editor whenever I have something important to communicate.

Next, I am thankful for my beautiful, smart, and talented daughters— Alana and Abrielle. They challenge me to be the best, every day of my life. Like my father always said, "Lead by example." Every day, I do what I do to show them that they can make their dreams come true.

My brother Sam Siegel and my sister Rose Siegel have always been among my strongest cheerleaders. They also do the hard work required to succeed in life. We are all more successful than we ever imagined.

My cousin Debbie Davis DDS, who also works for a nonprofit, helped by telling me people need to learn how to give. That insight set me on my current path. I can't thank her enough. My cousin Lisa Finerow has always reached out to family. My sister-in-law and brother-in-law, Lisa Pellegrino and Jeff Cogen, listened to my stories and dreams and encouraged me. I'll never forget the day they told me, "If anyone can do it, you can."

The next acknowledgement covers a wide range of people who've made a difference in my life and work. They include every colleague and assistant I have had over the years. Often, they were the ones who helped me with my spelling and grammar. I've always been good with the spoken word, but, without all of you and your support, I would not be producing this book today. There are too many of you to list. You know who you are, and I bow down to you for all your help.

A huge acknowledgement goes to my coaches along the way; most recently, my book coaches Susan Bender Phelps and Bonni Goldberg. Each of you has a gift with words and the structure to help me bring this book to the public. With your help, I clarified my message and delivered a book the world needs, and one I can be proud of. Thank you.

Another special acknowledgement goes to my executive coach, Victoria Trabosh. She helped me see the opportunity to create my own business and to have a greater impact on the world.

Thanks also to Andrew D'Addio, my business coach, who helped me put together a powerful business plan that guides me and gives me confidence. By following it, I am proving to my loving, supportive husband that this business is viable.

My first nonprofit manager, David Westcott, trusted my abilities and let me run with it. David always said, "Arlene, everything you do turns to GOLD." He encouraged me to become more involved in the Estate Planning Council of Portland by participating on the conference committee and board.

He was pleased that I was already a member of the Financial Planning Association of OR and SW Washington, and blessed my participation in the Northwest Planned Giving Roundtable (NWPGRT), a professional organization of fundraisers and planned giving practitioners. The nonprofit colleagues I have worked with at NWPGRT are the most collaborative I have ever encountered. Serving as secretary and then treasurer of that organization opened my world to professional relationships with individuals who generously provide me with a wealth of resources.

Of course, this book would not be possible if it weren't for all of the amazing individuals and families I had the honor of guiding on their philanthropic path. Every step of the way you showed success and leadership with love, compassion, courage, and hope for our future. Helping you achieve your legacy gave me happiness.

All of the professional advisors with whom I have worked over the years: estate planning attorneys, financial advisors, accountants and nonprofit professionals—it is impossible to list all of you. You trusted me and gave me the privilege of working with your top clients. A few key advisors I would like to mention include: Carolyn Miller, who let me educate her clients on philanthropy. She supports women entrepreneurs with a passion, and encouraged me when I went out on my own. Steve Kanter is an advisor who always includes philanthropy in his discussions with clients and sent newer attorneys to participate in my Mastermind groups. Michelle Castano Garcia trusted me with her top clients, sent colleagues to my Mastermind groups, and gave me incredible support when I opened my own business. She also played an instrumental role in this book.

Many times, the Oregon Community Foundation was a great choice for clients; other times, it was not. But, all charitable options are good for the client and the community. Together, we help people make a gift they perhaps could never have imagined making.

I also want to thank my Toastmasters and National Speakers Association colleagues who helped me hone my speaking skills. Yes, showing up and doing the hard work paid off. You inspire me, especially when the going gets tough.

Finally, to all the nonprofit boards and staff I work with, thank you for doing the good work. Thank you for trusting me to work with you to strengthen your organizations and to empower your missions.

This experience has shown me it takes a village to write a book. I am privileged to be part of a wonderful village. This book is built on my knowledge and expertise, and it is also the expression of my heart.

I want everyone to experience the joy of giving, "Money can buy you happiness, if you give it to a cause you care about."

CONTENTS

CHAPTER 1

HOW I GOT HERE AND WHY IT MATTERS

I grew up on Main Street, conquered Wall Street and, ultimately, returned to Main Street. It was a journey with some very unexpected twists and turns that tested me to my core and allowed me to grow and change in so many wonderful ways. The result is that my mission in life is to help everyone experience the joy of giving and to give a gift they never imagined possible.

It all began when I started my career on Wall Street. I worked for the very wealthy. My mission was to advise my clients, so that their money would grow, be retained, and passed to their heirs. I worked for some of the largest and best banks in the country: US Trust of NY, Citibank, and First Union (now Wells Fargo.) As a Certified Financial Planner (CFP)®[1], I had clients who loved getting richer and loved working with me. When I married Mitch Cogen, my clients sent us the most extravagant gifts we could ever have imagined.

In the spring of 1999, I was living in Connecticut with Mitch and our daughter, Alana. It was a busy time. With so many changes happening, we

---

1   The Certified Financial Planner™, CFP® and federally registered CFP (with flame design) marks (collectively, the "CFP® marks") are professional certification marks granted in the United States by the Certified Financial Planner Board of Standards, Inc.

started to reflect on our future. Mitch was working as an HR director while attending law school. He had just one more semester to complete before graduation. I was pregnant with our second daughter. I had preterm labor and was put on bed rest for the remainder of my pregnancy. My dad had passed away a few months earlier, so my mother was delighted to have something to take her mind off of it and came to stay with us to help.

All of these events led us to a life-altering decision. Neither Mitch nor I had grown up near extended family, and we realized that we wanted our children to have family nearby. Mitch's older brother Jeff and his wife Lisa were living in Portland, Oregon. They had two young children, and we had a toddler and a new baby on the way. Mitch really wanted to live closer to his brother. We both commented, "Wouldn't it be great to have our kids grow up together?" We took a leap of faith. We sold our house in Connecticut, quit our jobs, purchased a new home in Portland, and moved. When we arrived, Abrielle (Abby) was 10 days old, and Alana was 16 months old.

To add to the excitement and change, the move allowed me to stay home with the girls. Thankfully, Lisa became my best friend and introduced me to great friends and wonderful social opportunities. We took turns hosting weekly family dinners together and had play dates with our kids. Mitch still had to finish his last semester of law school, find a job, and pass the Oregon State Bar, but we were slowly getting settled into our new life.

Soon thereafter, Mitch graduated with honors, found a position with a great law firm, and passed the bar exam the first time. Then, Lisa went back to work, and I lost my partner in crime. But, I'd already made many new friends and the girls kept me busy, so things continued to go well.

One afternoon in June, less than 10 months into his new job, Mitch called me from work. It was late afternoon and the sun was shining. I was in the backyard playing with the girls on the new swing set.

Mitch said, "Honey, I am going to be home late."

Pause.

"What's going on, big case?" I asked.

"The partners have asked me out for drinks," he told me. "I think it's going to be very late before I get home." His excitement was bursting through the phone. This could only be good news. I was so happy and, honestly, not at all surprised. Mitch is the kind of person you want on your team. He is great partner material—smart, hardworking, and generous. I was smiling from ear to ear. This was a great opportunity.

But, when I hung up the phone, something didn't feel right. I was trembling. Mitch was a shining star at his firm. Lisa had landed a wonderful new job. I was so proud of them, but I was also so jealous. Being home with the girls was a privilege, yet something was missing for me. It wasn't what I'd expected, and I began to think that it was time for me to go back to work.

The problem was that I wasn't at all certain what I wanted to do. When I had worked on Wall Street, I was as successful as a woman could be. But, memories of the glass ceiling, sexual harassment, and wage discrimination made me feel exhausted. Things were changing, but very slowly. I didn't think I could go back to that kind of work. That is when Lisa recommended I see her career coach. She had found her very helpful and, as a result of their work together, Lisa had transitioned from working as an attorney to working as the Director at the Portland Children's Levy.

The career coach was also the right person for me. I was able to take my thoughts, dreams, and concerns to her as I contemplated my next career move. At the end of a very thoughtful and heart-wrenching process, I discovered that my core values were philanthropy and benevolence.

With this revelation, I looked my coach square in the eye and said, "Charity? Are you kidding me!? How do you make money working for a nonprofit?"

Needless to say, I had some concerns about this new direction. I knew that nonprofit salaries were relatively low. You get paid less money because you're doing the work of your heart. What's more, I couldn't see how my skill set would provide value in the nonprofit world. I also wanted to lead by example for my girls—Alana and Abby. I wanted them to know they could have a career they loved and fair compensation. Furthermore, I wanted them to know they could accomplish anything they put their minds to.

Even though I left my coach's office with a checklist of qualities for my next position, I was afraid and feeling insecure. I hadn't worked in more than two years. Doubts flashed through my mind as I began networking. Would anyone even want to hire me? I stayed in my comfort zone and met with lawyers, CPAs, several bankers, and investment people. I ended up jumping right back into the trust and investment world—maybe because, in this area, I knew I couldn't fail. During the following 5 years, I worked for a small local trust company and then a regional bank. But I still kept that career checklist posted in my office, and I looked at it every day.

I continued to ponder whether there was a position I would want at a nonprofit and whether there was one that paid well. Would I want to be an executive director, a programs person, or get involved in fundraising? Would I want to be at a large organization or a small one? Quite honestly, I wanted to do good *and* do well. That didn't look possible to me at that moment.

Five years later, I found the perfect charitable position for me. I became the Director of Gift Planning at the Oregon Community Foundation (OCF). OCF is the largest nonprofit in Oregon and the ninth largest community foundation in the country. My charge was to engage professional advisors and their clients in philanthropy. "Advisors are *my* people. I can do this."

My job would be to work with estate planning attorneys, accountants and financial advisors to educate and engage them in the giving process. The goal was to help them understand how the OCF was an excellent charitable resource for them and their clients. We wanted advisors to understand the impact the OCF had around the state. We wanted them to think of it as a resource for their clients who wanted to make a difference around the state.

In addition to educating professional advisors, I worked directly with individuals, families, and/or the boards of family foundations to help them clarify their values, find the right charitable causes, and choose the best charitable option(s) to make it all happen.

I was proud and happy with the work I was doing. Professionally, I was involved with the Estate Planning Council of Portland, the Financial Planning Association of Oregon and SW Washington, and the Northwest Planned Giving Roundtable (NWPGRT). Mitch was happy. I was happy. Life was good;

I was thinking I could stay here until I retire. There was no better nonprofit to be at in the state of Oregon.

Philanthropic Planning

In 2013, US Trust[2] released a study about philanthropic conversations and high-net-worth individuals. The study found that philanthropic conversations between professional advisors and their clients are important to have early and often. Of course, that is true, but here's where it gets interesting. While these discussions may have been taking place, they were falling short of their potential—a useful finding that I was sure to share with advisors.

High-net-worth individuals were looking to their advisors for more. They wanted to talk about fulfilling their philanthropic missions, involving the next generation, and leaving a lasting legacy. As part of these philanthropic goals, they needed more values-based discussions with their advisors—conversations that went beyond tax considerations and included life goals, values, and passions. Having these more complex conversations would make it possible for clients to attain their philanthropic ambitions for themselves, their families, and their communities.

I understood these findings to be the missing link. They confirmed my belief that my role at OCF could go beyond explaining the amazing benefits of giving. I could educate advisors, their clients, and individuals on how to discuss and set philanthropic goals.

In 2016, US Trust[3] published another study on high-net-worth philanthropy, and the results affirmed the conclusions of their earlier study. They detailed how philanthropic conversations between advisors and clients built deeper

---

2   "2013 U.S. Trust Insights On Wealth And Worth." *The WealthAdvisor*, US Trust, 2013, www.thewealthadvisor.com/article/us-trust-2013-insights-wealth-and-worth.

3   *High Net Worth Philanthropy Charitable Practices And Preferences Of Wealthy Households.* Bank of America , 2016, pp. 1–114, *High Net Worth Philanthropy Charitable Practices And Preferences Of Wealthy Households.*

relationships. Interestingly, they also found that philanthropic conversations had a unique ability to engage the next generation in the giving process.

The results of these studies highlighted an important opportunity that was being overlooked—planning and talking about philanthropic goals. This realization also set me on the path to helping people understand the amazing impact giving can have on themselves and their community.

As you start to think about this process, here are some ways you can begin planning:

1. If you haven't included philanthropy in your estate planning or overall financial plan, I highly recommend you call your advisors and your family members to begin that conversation. If you have included philanthropy, but haven't engaged your family, this would be a great time to get that process started.

2. When deciding which charities to give to, you and your financial advisor may want to consider working with your local community foundation. One of the benefits of working with a community foundation is their neutrality and the breadth of knowledge they can provide. Clients/donors can explore giving opportunities related to their passions and interests, like education, the arts, health care, animals, landowner rights, the environment, and more. Community foundations don't compete with financial advisors; rather, they serve as a resource for everyone.

3. Whatever the size of your estate, there are financial tools that will help you take care of your loved ones and allow you to leave a legacy to the cause that touches your heart. By getting your family engaged in the conversation early on with your financial advisor, you can more easily navigate the tensions that many families experience around inheritance issues.

I worked at OCF for nine years. It's the longest I've ever been with any organization. My motto during that time was, "Dream job; life is good; I can't complain." The Oregon Community Foundation gave me the opportunity to delve deeper into the practice of philanthropy and develop a suite of skills, knowledge, and expertise that I could eventually use to go out on my own. When I started, I had no idea my work would change my own giving—and my family—in the most wonderful way possible.

My Personal Giving Story

On May 5, 2010, my mother called. "Arlene, I have something important to tell you," and then she choked back a tear. I'll never forget that moment. "I just came from the doctor's office. My tests came back positive for pancreatic cancer."

At best, she'd have six to eight months. We got seven with our mom. My sister, Rose, brother, Sam, and I took turns going to Florida to stay with her. It was the toughest thing I'd faced since we'd lost my dad 13 years earlier. Yet, during that time, we had some of our most beautiful and meaningful conversations.

On my first visit, as soon as I put my luggage down, my mom handed me a stack of papers, and said, "Ok, my financial expert daughter, look over my estate plan and tell me what you think."

If you knew my mom, you'd know she liked to get straight to business. Before we went through her medical update, she wanted me to read the documents and make sure that, after charity, her money was divided equally between the three of us. So, that's what I did. I sat down, read the documents, and confirmed that after charity, it was divided equally. She was so relieved.

While reviewing the documents, I noticed only 5% of her estate was going to charity, and it surprised me. When I pointed it out to Mom, she told me she thought 5% was a lot of money to give away. When I showed her plan to Rose and Sam and shared my concern, they agreed that she should feel free to give more. When our dad was alive, they always generously supported different causes in our community, though not nearly as generously as she could be now. Together, we encouraged Mom to give more to charity. She increased the charitable portion of her estate to 10%.

At first, she was hesitant, but you should have seen her face when she was deciding where to give the additional 5%. Her eyes lit up. "Oh, I'll give a little more to B'nai Torah (her synagogue), and a little more to the Jewish Federation. They do so much." She was like a kid in a candy store. I well up every time I think of that moment.

When my mother chose to give only to Jewish organizations, I was surprised. I asked her why, and she reminded me of what author, human rights activist, and Holocaust survivor, Elie Wiesel said, "Only Jews give to Jewish organizations." As it turns out, when I checked the data (I'm a show-me kind of person), I learned that **all** major gifts to Jewish charities are made by Jewish people.

Among the more meaningful gifts my mother made was the gift to her synagogue. It was the largest gift B'nai Torah ever received. She created an education fund, something she would never have imagined she would be able to do. The goal of the fund is to keep the congregation, especially the kids, engaged in Judaism.

Like so many of the people I worked with through my job at the Oregon Community Foundation, my mom waited until the end of her life to experience the joy of significant giving. As I thought of the hundreds of people I'd worked with to create funds that would activate after someone's death, I had the profound realization that we had all missed something very important. This realization would alter the course of my life.

It was beautiful and painful to watch my mother go through cancer. Each time I came to visit, we would go to doctor's appointments and treatments. We would talk, and she would ask questions.

"So, what are *you* going to do with the money?" she asked.

"You mean the inheritance?" I countered.

"Yes, the money." she rebutted, once again getting straight to business.

"It's simple Mom. I am going to do three things:

　　1) Create a donor-advised fund

　　2) Bring the family to Israel

　　3) Invest the rest to go towards the girls' education."

Each represented a value she passed onto me. Be generous, Israel matters, and provide an education for your children.

After my mother died, we created a donor-advised fund with part of the inheritance. Several of my friends questioned why we would create a fund like this when we had two teenagers about to go off to college. They told us to wait, that the money could be a year's tuition. I understood their concerns, but we had planned for our girls' education and the $25,000 donation to create that fund was not going to prevent our girls from going to college. More importantly, in collaboration with Mitch and the girls, creating that fund was one of the most satisfying things we ever did together.

The four of us sat down in the Oregon Community Foundation conference room with one of my colleagues, our donor relationship officer, Kirsten Kilchenstein. This was new for the family, so I just sat there and let them engage. She asked us the same questions I'd asked so many families over the years. When she asked, "How would you like your fund invested—in the main pool or the socially responsible investment pool?"

Our youngest, Abby, stated with absolute certainty, "Social, of course, why would we choose differently?"

Mitch and I looked at each other, shrugged our shoulders and agreed with Abby. In considering our first grant, we chose to focus on education. Both of our girls attended Lincoln High School. We thought this would be a great way to give back. As Mitch and I were poised to fill out the paperwork to finalize our gift, Alana asked, "Why would we give to Lincoln? It's a wealthy school; they have a lot of money. Why wouldn't we give to a school in greater need?"

Mitch and I looked at each other and said at the same time, "Why don't we do both?"

The girls loved the idea. Kirsten researched the high schools in our district with the highest levels of need, based on free and reduced lunch rates. We chose Roosevelt High School and structured the gift so they could use it where they most needed it.

That day, Mitch and I developed a whole new appreciation for our daughters and the caring and compassionate women they had become. We'd always been proud of them, but we discovered that giving together opened a new world for all of us. We got to look into each other's hearts in a new and powerful way.

We also used some of the inheritance to take our daughters to Israel, as I told my mother we would do. We had an amazing time. We hiked Masada, travelled to the West Bank, and visited Jerusalem. As for their education, Alana and Abby are both in college, and we are happily paying for it.

Having been an advisor for years, I know that more than anything, advisors want to add value for their clients. They want to build a deeper relationship with you and get to know your family. In order for them to add value, your advisors need to know your difficulties, desires, and dreams. The more the advisor knows about you, your family, and your business, the more value-driven strategies they can incorporate into your plan, so you can attain your goals. Having philanthropic conversations with your professional advisor helps you to create a more holistic plan. In the process, you get to create a legacy and leave a gift you never imagined possible.

My experiences have demonstrated, time and time again, that successful families tend to pass down values—and that philanthropy is a great way to help sustain those values. For more than a decade, I have been privileged to help hundreds of individuals, couples, and families integrate philanthropy into their plans in ways they never imagined. Many of them find philanthropy can solve personal problems and tax problems at the same time.

There were individuals and couples who were the last of their line, and I helped them create beautiful tributes to their loved ones and their passions. Their stories are in the following chapters. They will allow you to get a focused view of how we use the many tools and techniques that are already in place. These tools can help you engage and give a gift you never imagined and/or help you to create a legacy. It's my hope that these stories will inspire you to do the same.

The Right Mindset

As you read, keep in mind that in order to use philanthropy for happiness and significance, you will want to start with the right mindset. There are three foundational perspectives you will need:

1. Everyone involved is already starting from a successful situation.

2. You are or want to be an active member of the community.

3. We will use the Five Levels of Maslow's Hierarchy of Needs as a guide, working at the very top of the triangle with self–actualization (achieving your inner potential). This is the pinnacle of life—the level you and your advisor are aiming at through philanthropy.

SELF ACTUALIZATION
Fulfillment, inner potential, experience purpose and meaning

SELF - ESTEEM
Achievement, mastery recognition and respect

LOVE & BELONGING
Friends, family, intimacy and community

SAFETY & SECURITY
Security, health, employment and freedom from fear

PHYSIOLOGICAL NEEDS
Food, water, shelter and rest

Maslow's Hierarchy of Needs

[4]

---

4   **Maslow**, A. H. (**1943**). A theory of human motivation. Psychological Review, 50(4), 370-396.

Using these perspectives to frame your choices, you will be able to engage your children and generations to come while making a difference in your community.

I hope this book will provide you with a new perspective on philanthropy, financial planning, making a difference, and so much more. It is my hope that you take the opportunity to engage your children in new ways to think about giving and pass down or create new family values. Learn from these stories— how you can use philanthropy to solve personal and financial challenges, or how to leave a legacy far greater than you ever imagined … just like my mother.

Amen. Hallelujah!

CHAPTER 2

WHY WE GIVE TO LIVE

Reasons for Giving

Everywhere you look, there is need. It's hard to overlook the problems of the world—people are suffering; opportunities and justice are withheld; schools, colleges, and universities need support; animals are in danger and habitats are threatened; and incurable diseases still strike down our loved ones. And then, there are the disasters, both natural and manmade. The list is never-ending, and it appears there will never be enough resources to address all of these serious issues.

It may surprise you to know that most donors are NOT discouraged by the seemingly insurmountable odds. Take a look at these giving statistics from Giving USA's 2018 Annual Report on Philanthropy for 2017:[5]

---

5   USA, Giving. "Giving USA 2018: Americans Gave $410.02 Billion to Charity in 2017, Crossing the $400 Billion Mark for the First Time." *Giving USA 2017: Total Charitable Donations Rise to New High of $390.05 Billion | Giving USA*, 2018, givingusa.org/.

Giving USA 2018

Total : **410 billion**

127.37 billion	**31%**	Religion
58.90 billion	**14%**	Education
50.06 billion	**12%**	Human Services
45.89 billion	**11%**	Foundations
38.27 billion	**9%**	Health
29.59 billion	**7%**	Public Society Benefit
19.51 billion	**5%**	Arts Culture and Humanities
22.97 billion	**6%**	International Affairs
11.83 billion	**3%**	Environment and Animals
7.87 billion	**2%**	Other

Source: Giving USA 2018 https://givingusa.org/tag/giving-usa-2018/

We are either a nation of wide-eyed optimists, or we get something truly valuable from giving. It's probably a combination of the two. And, we have results from some very impressive research that prove we are happier when we give to help another (and so are people who give in other countries).

Giving USA also provides us information on where the giving comes from. Amazingly, 70% of that $410 billion (more than $286 billion) comes from individuals/families.

Science of Giving

In 2008, Michael Norton, an associate business professor at Harvard, conducted a study on money and happiness. Based on the study, he gave a Ted Talk, "How to Buy Happiness," that is available online and is worth watching.

The study began with Canadian college students who volunteered to participate in an experiment[6]. The individuals who participated were asked to rate how happy they were. Then, they were given an envelope with either $5 or $20 inside. Those who received $5 were instructed to spend the money on themselves, and those with $20 were asked to spend the money on others. At the end of the day, someone would call them to follow up on their experience.

Those who received $5, for the most part, bought themselves a coffee. They reported no change in how they felt. Those who spent the $20 on others, though, reported they felt happier at the end of the day.

Norton also looked at a Gallup organization survey conducted using similar experiments in other countries. Even with different populations, they got the same results: spending money to do something for someone else creates a greater sense of happiness than spending money on oneself. This study—which was conducted across 136 countries with over 200,000 participants—included a question about recent charitable donations and life satisfaction. In 120 of the countries, individuals who had donated money to charity within the last month reported greater satisfaction with their life than those who hadn't given. These survey results show that the positive correlation between giving money to charity and happiness seems to be universal.

Professor Norton concludes that if you think money can't buy you happiness, you're not spending it in the right way. In other words, one route to greater happiness may be to spend less money on yourself and instead spend it to help other people. Norton's research demonstrates the direct correlation between giving money to others and happiness. In my opinion, this means you really *can* buy a stairway to heaven (thank you, Led Zeppelin).

Another study, from 2006, conducted by neuroscientist Dr. Jorge Moll, head of D'Or Institute for Research and Education in Rio de Janeiro, Brazil, arrived at the same conclusion, but in a very different way. His team used functional magnetic resonance imaging (MRI) to study participants while they anonymously donated to real charitable organizations connected to

---

6   Norton, Michael, et al. "Spending Money on Others Promotes Happiness." *Science*, 21 Mar. 2008.

major societal causes. The MRIs showed that the mesolimbic pathway, or reward system in the brain, engaged the same way when the participants made their donation as it does when one receives a monetary reward. The results demonstrated that when you put others' interest before your own, your act of generosity activates the prefrontal cortex—the part of the brain that usually lights up in response to sex and food.

I remember the look of joy on my mother's face when she increased the amount of money she gave to causes that were important to her. And, when I think about my own family's story of giving a significant portion of the money she left us, I can say these experiences mirror what the studies found. The bottom line is, we feel good—really good—and we are happier when we give.

Three Areas of Planning

To get you started on the road to this good feeling, there are three areas you should address with your advisors:

Comprehensive/Holistic Planning

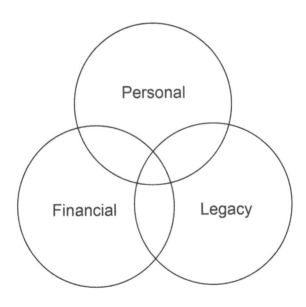

**

Personal

The first area to consider is the personal side of giving. Many of the families I've worked with wanted to give to charity, but also wanted to be able to take care of loved ones. You'll be happy to know that you can do both. We have some wonderfully creative tools to help you care for a loved one with disabilities or provide an income for a family member throughout their life. Once that person reaches the end of their life, any remaining money goes to the charitable cause of your choice. Through the stories that follow, you will get a clearer picture of how people just like you used these tools and incorporated philanthropy during their lives and beyond.

Financial

The second area is your financial picture. There are a couple of key aspects to consider.

Tax benefits—Even though US tax laws have recently changed, the good news is that philanthropy still has some very attractive tax benefits. Your financial advisor can give you the best advice regarding your specific situation.

Wealth preservation from one generation to another—It's important to work with your advisor to implement a plan that will help ensure your assets are sustained for the future. In the US, the first generation retains 100% of their wealth. The second generation retains about 30% of their family wealth, and the third generation only maintains about 10% of family wealth.[7],[8],[9]

---

7   Ward, John L. *A Family Business Publication*. Palgrave Macmillan US, 2011.

8   Economist , the. "The New Wealth of Nations." *The Economist*, The Economist Newspaper, 2001, special-report/2001/06/14/the-new-wealth-of-nations.

9   Beckhard, Richard, and W. Gibb Dyer. "Managing Continuity in the Family-Owned Business." Sciencedirect, Elsevier, 2 Dec. 2003, www.sciencedirect.com/science/article/pii/0090261683900220.

Many countries and cultures preserve little or no family wealth at all. In the US, the saying is "From shirtsleeves to shirtsleeves in three generations." We didn't make that up, we just rephrased it.

For more than 2,000 years the saying in China has been, "Wealth never survives three generations." Mexico's phrase is "First generation traders, second generation gentleman, and third generation beggars." In Italy, it's, "From stalls to stars to stalls." Ireland's saying is "Clogs to clogs in three generations." And, in India, they say "Peasant's shoes to peasant's shoes in three generations."

I would love to learn if your country has a similar phrase. Please share it in an email to Arlene@ArleneCogen.com and put **3 Generations** in the subject line.

Legacy

The third piece is your legacy. Just like the Rockefellers, Buffetts, and my mother, you, too, can leave a legacy through philanthropy. Some questions you should ask when considering how you want to be remembered, include:

- What do I want to be remembered for?
- What values, life lessons, and stories shaped my life?
- How do I want others to benefit from those lessons?
- How do I want to honor a loved one?
- What do I want to change in the world?
- What do I love and want to ensure continues in the world?

You may not know the answers to these questions right now. But, thinking through them can be the first step of your philanthropic journey. Some of the families I've worked with answered these questions before they came to work with me. More often, it was a lengthy process of meeting with me, meeting with family members, and researching the different organizations and institutions whose missions matched their goals. One family took more than a decade to finalize their plans. While most complete the process more quickly, thoughtful philanthropy takes time, practice, and focus. As a philanthropic consultant, I provide a framework, information, insight, and ideas about philanthropy, so you can move from awareness to action.

CHAPTER 3

GIVING DURING OR AFTER YOUR LIFE

When Will You Give

One of the first choices you will make is whether you want to make charitable gifts during or after your life. If your financial resources permit, you may decide that you would like to do both. There are advantages to each and a variety of tools to accomplish your goals. The options discussed below can help start your thoughts. Your financial advisor can answer questions and help guide your decisions.

Giving While Alive

You can make outright gifts to charity throughout your life. Many of you have been doing so since you were children. You've dropped coins in a jar at the grocery store, bought Girl Scout cookies or magazines from your neighbors' kids, or gone to the school car wash. You also may have participated in walks and Go-Fund-Me causes. You've contributed to the church collection plate, supported a local school, your college or university, or a local, national, or international charity. Perhaps you've contributed after a disaster. These donations go directly to the organization to support their mission and the good works they do.

Other ways that people give during their life include forming a private family charitable foundation, partnering with an existing charitable foundation to create a donor-advised fund, and/or creating a split-interest gift that allows you to care for a loved one who cannot take care of themselves (for as long as they live) with the remainder going to a charity of your choice.

These options allow you to solve problems, retain wealth, reduce tax liability, and make a difference—all while giving you (and perhaps other family members) the opportunity to feel the deep happiness that giving to others brings. If you are able to give a significantly large gift, the amount of that gift is removed from your estate and may result in lowering estate taxes for your heirs.

Giving After Your Life

Estate planning allows you to make your charitable gifts after you die. There are many options to help you do that in a thoughtful way. You miss out on being able to see, firsthand, the difference your gift makes, but can still feel good because of the legacy your careful planning allows you to leave. It could be naming something after you or a family member—a wing of your favorite hospital, a building on the campus of your alma mater, research or educational grants, and so much more.

Financial Tools for Giving

On the following pages, you will find descriptions of different financial tools you may be able to use in order to give charitably during your lifetime or through your estate plan. Once you're familiar with the full range of options, you can meet with your financial advisors, CPAs, and estate planning attorneys to choose the tool or tools that will be right for you and your situation.

Outright Gifts

An outright gift is the most common and simplest type of giving. Outright gifts can include cash, marketable securities, real estate, business interests, and even cryptocurrency. From a legal perspective, you can only give a gift if you own what you are giving away and have the mental capacity to do so. The gift must be delivered, received, and accepted. Please keep in mind that not all charities are able to accept all types of assets.

Giving an outright gift during your lifetime allows you to experience the joy associated with helping others. It also removes the asset from your estate for tax purposes. However, there are also some disadvantages to outright giving while still alive. First, you no longer own the property and, thereby, forfeit all control. Second, the property may appreciate over time, and you will not benefit from that growth. Third, different assets have different tax deductibility. This is why you need to bring your advisors into your decision-making process. They can talk you through the different situations and help you determine which is the most tax-favored way to make a gift, as well as which assets to use.

You can also make an outright gift after you die. Your will or trust would identify your desired gifts to charities. Of course, as with the gifts made during your life, there are also advantages and disadvantages to giving an outright gift after you die.

The advantages include the fact that you get full use of the asset during your whole lifetime, and you still get to direct who receives your gift—whether it is an individual or a charity. Also, if you wait and give through your will, there may be different tax advantages for you and/or the recipient.

Among the disadvantages of making an outright gift after you die is the fact that you miss out on the great feeling of happiness that results from helping make a difference. Additionally, the opportunity to use a more tax advantaged asset may be lost. And, if the recipient is an individual, it's possible that they may predecease you and never receive the gift.

Bequests

A bequest is an excellent way to include a charity in your estate plan. A bequest can be in a will, living trust, or with a codicil or amendment. Bequests make up 80% of all legacy gifts and are approximately 7% of all giving.

There are four types of bequests.

1. **Specific Bequest.** A specific bequest is when you make a gift of a specific dollar amount or other property. For example, you may wish to leave $10,000 to your favorite cause.

2. **Percentage Bequest.** The percentage bequest involves leaving a specific percentage of your overall estate to a charity. For example, you may wish to leave 10% of your estate to community libraries. These gifts are calculated based on the value of your estate when you die, and typically result in larger gifts to the nonprofit.

3. **Residual Bequest.** A residual bequest is the balance of an estate after the will or trust has given to each of the specific and percentage bequests. A common residual bequest involves leaving the residue (remaining portion) of the estate to charity. For example, you may wish to leave the residue of your estate to a donor-advised fund—I will talk about these later in the chapter. A donor-advised fund is a terrific vehicle to engage multiple generations in philanthropy. A memorable residual bequest was given to OCF while I worked there. We received the largest single gift ever made to OCF, via a residual bequest from Fred Fields, owner of Coe Industries, of over $150 million. In 2012, that was one of the largest single gifts made to any community foundation in the country.

4. **Contingent Bequest.** A contingent bequest is made to charity only if the purpose of the primary bequest cannot be met. For example, you could leave specific property, such as a vacation home, to a relative, but the bequest language could provide that if the relative is not alive at the time of your death, the vacation home will go to a charity.

In order to include a bequest in your plan you will need to see an attorney to draft your will, trust, and other critical estate planning documents. You will incur legal fees for the initial draft, as well as any subsequent changes.

Beneficiary Designation—Operation of Law

The beneficiary designation is a quick, efficient way to include philanthropy in your plan. This section focuses specifically on retirement account beneficiaries.

When you withdraw money from a qualified retirement plan, it is subject to income taxes. This is also true for any individual beneficiaries or heirs who receive funds after you pass away. They will be responsible for the income tax.

On the other hand, a retirement plan can be a tax-efficient and simple way to figure philanthropy into your estate plan. You can make a charity (or charities) the beneficiary for all or part of the value.

Key Concept
- You leave money to charity at death

Benefits
- You have complete control of the asset during your lifetime
- Asset is removed from estate at death for tax purposes

Challenges
- What are the best assets to use?

Key principle
- Leave tax-burdened assets (e.g., retirement assets) to charity and leave tax-favored assets to family. See your advisor to help make these decisions.

Ideally, it should be relatively simple to include a charity as a beneficiary in your estate plan. You can usually get the form from your retirement plan administrator or the human resources department of your company.

If your retirement account is administered by a financial advisor, you can call them to ask for a beneficiary designation form or may even be able to download the form from their website.

Once you've updated your form to add a charity as a beneficiary, return it and be sure to get an acknowledgement that it was updated. This will not cost you anything, and you will feel good knowing you've planned for sustained support of a cause that's important to you.

Other accounts that operate by law and have a separate form to complete to identify the beneficiary directly are:

- Payable on Death (POD) accounts: CDs, brokerage accounts
- Life insurance policies
- Individual retirement plans (IRAs)
- Qualified retirement plans (401(k), 403(b))
- Profit sharing plans

Your financial advisor can help you determine which, if any, of these make sense for you.

Planned Gifts and Split-Interest Gifts

The next category of giving to consider is a planned gift. These gifts are often more substantial amounts, but don't necessarily have to be. With a planned gift, you will generally work with several different professionals to generate the best plan. Your accountant will help figure out the tax implications, and your financial advisor can help determine which asset (or assets) to use for the gift. Your attorney will make sure your wishes are fulfilled in a legal manner. You may also choose to include a philanthropic advisor or someone from the charity in the discussions about your planned gift.

There is a misconception that you need to be wealthy to make a planned gift. While they are sometimes large gifts, that is not always the case, and planned gifts can be made during your life or through your estate plan.

If you have significant assets at your disposal, and a loved one who may need financial support throughout their life, you can consider making a specific type of planned gift called a split-interest gift. With these, you are able to provide an income stream to a loved one who is unable to care for themselves. Then, when they die, the remaining money goes to the charity you chose when you set up the gift. This kind of gift can provide solutions for both your immediate and extended family, allows you to experience the happiness of giving, and may reduce or eliminate some tax burdens.

Charitable Gift Annuities

A charitable gift annuity is a simple contract between you and a charity. As a donor, you make an irrevocable or completed gift to charity. The terms of the contract sate that for your gift, you or a loved one(s) will receive a fixed stream of income from the charity for the rest of their life.

Rates for the income stream are suggested by the ACGA. The ACGA is the American Council on Gift Annuities. The ACGA uses actuarial tables to determine annuity rates, and the majority of nonprofits use these rates to simplify giving. This means you can give from your heart and give to a cause you care about instead of shopping for a better rate.

Both the annuity payout rate and tax deduction calculations are actuarially based, using the Applicable Federal Rates (AFR). The calculation assumes 50% of the original gift will go to charity after the annuitant dies. The AFR is published monthly by the IRS.

Gift of Cash or Marketable Securities

Charitable Gift Annuity

Summary of the key aspects of gift annuities

- They're irrevocable gifts—once given, you cannot have them back.
- They provide immediate, partial tax deductions for the gift. Since you receive an income stream from the annuity, you cannot take a tax deduction on that portion. Your partial tax deduction is calculated based on the estimated future value of the remainder interest that will go to charity.
- They provide higher rates of return than certificates of deposit.
- They can be funded with cash or appreciated securities.
- They are split-interest gifts.
- The annuitant gets an income stream, and the remainder goes to charity.

Benefits

- Charity pays fixed amount to annuitant for life.
- Simple contract
- Entry-level gift for you if you love an organization
- Removes asset from your estate
- One or joint annuitant(s)

Challenges

- Charitable Gift Annuities (CGAs) are based on the financial strength of the nonprofit organization (NPO). Do your due diligence with the NPO. If they run out of money, you do too.
- Cannot gift business interests, artwork, or any unusual asset.
- There are specific age requirements to set up a gift annuity.
- The fixed income for life may not keep pace with inflation.
- You cannot support multiple charities. You must set up multiple gift annuities, one for each charity.
- There is typically no aftermarket, meaning the annuitant can't sell, close, or cash out the annuity.
- Payments are lower than a commercial gift annuity (the type offered by a life insurance company or investment firm) because the primary purpose is nonprofit support.

There are three types of charitable gift annuities: immediate, deferred, and flexible. They all share the basic characteristics outlined above, but the initiation of the income stream varies.

With immediate annuities, payments to the annuitant begin immediately, and the remainder goes to chartiy.

For deferred annuities, income stream payments to the annuitant begin at a specific point in time, which has been detailed in the contract.

Flexible annuities have multiple start dates.

With each of these annuity types, payments to you are taxed in a favorable manner:

- Part ordinary income
- Part capital gains
- Part tax free

Murphy's Law of charitable gift annuities states: if you create one, you will outlive your life expectancy.

Charitable Remainder Trust (CRT)

A charitable remainder trust is created by your attorney, and generates income for loved ones and can enable you to pursue your philanthropic goals. Charitable remainder trusts require a Taxpayer Identification Number and are therefore a separate entity for investment and tax purposes. You, as the settlor, identify the trustee, beneficiary, and charitable remainder, and determine the payout rate and period of time for the trust. You will need to see an attorney to draft a charitable remainder trust, so there are costs associated with setting up this type of trust. In addition, each year you will need to fill out a separate tax return and manage the assets.

Charitable trusts offer flexibility and control over your intended charitable beneficiaries and provide lifetime income. That lifetime income can help with retirement, estate planning, and tax management, while still ensuring an appropriate inheritance.

The investments within a charitable trust account cannot be comingled with other assets. Payments are a set percentage and are based on the year-end value of the trust. They are paid out to you in the next year. If invested well, this type of charitable gift can keep pace with inflation.

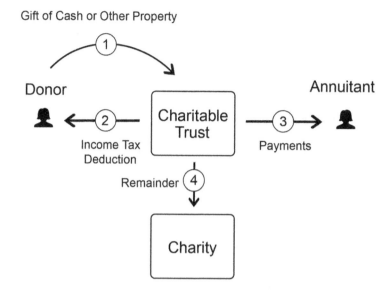

Charitable Remainder Trust

Summary of the key aspects of charitable remainder trusts

- They're an irrevocable gift—once given, you cannot have them back.
- They provide an immediate tax deduction for a percentage of the gift. Since you receive an income stream from the trust, you cannot take a tax deduction on the money you receive. You do get a deduction on the future value of the estimated remainder that will go to charity.
- They are split-interest gifts.
- The beneficiary gets an income stream for life, no more than 20 years, or a combination of both.
- The remainder goes to charity.

Benefits

- May be funded with a wide range of assets: cash, marketable securities, business interests, real estate and certain other complex assets.

- Assets are invested in a diversified portfolio.
- May have multiple beneficiaries
- May receive additional gifts
- Removes asset from estate
- May be funded with appreciated assets to reduce capital gains

Challenges

- Payout determined by donor; which may not be sustainable. Four-tier order for distribution of income
  - o Ordinary Income
  - o Capital gains income—short term first, then long term
  - o Tax-exempt income (or other)
  - o Distribution of principal (tax-exempt)

Given the costs to create and maintain a CRT, I recommend you consider starting with a minimum of $100,000. Many trust companies and charities can act as trustee on your behalf.

In some instances, the remainder of a charitable trust can be directed to a donor-advised fund.

Donor-Advised Fund

A donor-advised fund is a wonderful charitable vehicle to help with your philanthropy. They are one of the fastest growing charitable vehicles in the country. Donor-advised funds are administered by a public charity on behalf of an individual, family, or business. You can also create a donor-advised fund with a sponsoring organization, such as a national or community charity.

The donor-advised fund is a component fund or account that is maintained and operated by the sponsoring organization. Donor-advised funds typically have no set up costs, have low ongoing expenses, and are not assessed additional taxes on the income earned in the fund.

Donor-advised funds are established at public grantmaking charities, which improve the lives of people in their community. These organizations bring together financial resources, research, and community outreach to support effective nonprofits in the community.

A donor–advised fund is an agreement between the donor and the sponsoring organization. The agreement allows the donor to recommend grants for distribution to other charities. Donor-advised funds are like mini private foundations. You receive all the fun of philanthropy without the administrative hassles. The national or community foundation charities handle the administration of the fund on your behalf. This administration includes (but is not limited to) creating a fund, making policies about investing the assets, preparing tax returns, providing due diligence on the nonprofit organizations, and more.

Donor-advised funds are very simple to create. The national/community charity provides the paperwork for your fund, and you sign the document. Once the paperwork is complete, you make an irrevocable contribution to the fund. You then immediately receive the maximum tax deduction allowable by the IRS. The community foundation or institution manages the investments and administers the fund. Any growth in the fund is tax-free. Once the fund is established, you can make recommendations for grantmaking to qualified charities. Grants can be made to 501(c)(3), organizations—religious or public—and can be made anonymously.

Most donor-advised funds can also help individuals and families create a legacy. This is accomplished by identifying successor advisors for the fund. The number of successor advisors allowed varies per charitable organization. Work with your advisor to determine which charitable structure will help you achieve your goals.

For example, if the charity limits successor advisors to two generations, you either create the fund during your life, and your children will be the successor advisors, or you create the fund through your estate plan, making your children the initial advisors and your grandchildren the successor advisors.

Most donor-advised funds are created by a gift of cash or marketable securities. Gifts of appreciated property avoid capital gains if held more than one year. With due diligence and acceptance, charities may accept gifts of real property, LLCs, and more. Current tax laws prohibit IRA required minimum distributions during your life to fund a donor-advised fund. However, retirement account assets can be transferred to a donor advised fund at death. Retirement assets bequeathed to a charity avoid both estate and income tax.

A donor-advised fund offers the opportunity to create an efficient, low-cost vehicle that is easy to establish and very flexible. It can be a wonderful alternative to giving directly to charity or creating a private foundation.

Benefits of donor-advised funds

- Simple and flexible
- Immediate charitable deduction at the time of your donation
- You recommend which qualified charitable organizations to support
- You receive maximum tax advantages
- Donor-advised funds are exempt from estate taxes
- Contributions to donor-advised fund through your estate are not subject to estate taxes
- You can be anonymous
- Consolidates giving—no longer need to track receipts
- Creates a family legacy
- Your money manager may be able to manage the investments in your charitable fund.
- Donor-advised funds may be permanent, wholly expendable, or spent down over a period of time.

Challenges of donor-advised funds

- Account minimums may vary from $5,000 to $50,000.
- You cannot satisfy a personal pledge to a charity from a donor-advised fund.
- You can suggest which charities receive contributions, but the sponsoring organization makes the final decision on recipients.

- You, as the donor, cannot receive personal benefits (e.g., tickets to a dinner or event).

- Money cannot be used to contribute to a political party or candidate.

Your financial advisor can help you explore how a donor-advised fund might work for you and your family.

Donor-Directed or Legacy Fund

A donor-directed fund, also known as a legacy fund, allows you to support an organization (or organizations) in perpetuity. This is also called an endowment. Endowments are financial assets that are donated and are meant to be invested to grow the principal and provide income for future investing and expenditures. Typically, endowment funds have a strict set of long-term guidelines dictating the asset allocation that will yield the targeted return without taking on too much risk.

In the donor-directed fund agreement, you name specific nonprofits you want to receive a percentage of the annual distribution each year. If an organization should cease to exist, its share can be divided among the remaining organizations on your list.

Endowing an annual gift is a simple calculation. Let's say that every year you give a gift of $100 to your favorite charity. In order for them to receive that $100 gift when you are no longer alive, take your annual gift and multiple it by 20 to get $2,000.00. If you leave $2,000 in an endowment gift to the organization, then, if invested well with a typical 5% annual payout, your charity will continue to receive its $100 each year in perpetuity.

If you want to continue your support for a number of organizations, a donor-directed fund can simplify your estate plan. Your will or trust directs the charitable portion of your estate to the directed fund. The directed fund that is on file with the charitable organization can be changed or modified while you are alive and competent. Like a donor-advised fund, a donor-directed fund consolidates your giving into one place to ensure effective investment management of the fund. There is no cost to update the fund agreement.

Private Foundations

Private foundations are usually supported financially by one or more sources, like an individual, a family, or a corporation. They are required by IRS rules to give out 5% of their assets each year in grants and require a setup process that can be time consuming and costly.

They can be a good option if you are interested in the whole process of giving, and you have a lot of money. Private foundations can range in size from $100,000 to billions of dollars. You can talk to your advisor to see what an appropriate amount is for a private foundation where you live. When I lived in New York, you needed a minimum of $20 million to create a private foundation. In Oregon, the minimum number is $5 million.

Key concept

- With a private foundation, the donor has ultimate control.

Benefits

- Private foundations allow successor generations to participate. The client/donor has total control over asset management and grant distributions. They also have the ability to hire staff to perform these duties.

Challenges

Creating a private foundation can be costly. There are costs associated with drafting the legal and governance documents necessary to become a private foundation with tax-deductible status. Other areas that incur ongoing expenses include legal, investment management and accounting services. The grantmaking process may require support or staff as well. Certain foundations allow hiring of family members for different administrative roles.

As you can see, you have a number of ways to create a legacy. It can be through a private foundation or a donor-advised or directed fund. With a solid financial plan that incorporates philanthropy, the tools described in this chapter can help you understand how you can create and manage charitable funds. Your advisors can help you determine the best vehicle for you and your family.

If you are considering what type of charitable vehicle to use, below is a comparison chart of private foundations and donor funds. This chart compares administrative, tax and control issues for private foundations and donor funds.[10]

Private Foundation and Donor Funds Comparison Chart

	Private Foundation	Donor Advised Fund (DAF)	Donor Designated Fund (DDF)
Tax Status	Private Charity	Public Charity	Public Charity
Start up time	Can take weeks or months to create and receive 501(c)(3) charitable status	Immediate	Immediate
Total limit for all annual contributions	30% of Adjusted Gross Income	60% of Adjusted Gross Income	60% of Adjusted Gross Income
Tax Filings	Prepare own 990 PF with supporting schedules	Accounts are considered component funds of the charity and are included in the foundation 990	Accounts are considered component funds of the charity and are included in the foundation 990
Costs to set up	Several thousand dollars in legal accounting fees and filing expenses	None	None
Contribution	Varies, $5+ million	Minimums as low as $5,000	Minimums may apply and vary
Retain Financial Advisor	Yes	Varies, if they do, minimum requirements apply	Varies, if they do, minimum requirements apply
Privacy	Required to file tax returns on grants, investment fee, staff salaries, etc. These are public records and are compiled into grant seeker's directories	Individual donors and or the grants they make can be kept private if the donor wishes	Individual donors and or the grants they make can be kept private if the donor wishes
Control	Donor	Charitable Organization	Charitable Organization
Required annual distribution	5% annual	Varies, some have no requirement	Varies, some have no requirement
Family Engagement	Yes, unlimited participation	May have limitations, check requirements at charitable organization	None

Gifting Sources

Annual giving is made from pocket change, or you've worked it into your budget. There are no surprises, and you are happy to participate. It could be a membership subscription, like Oregon Public Broadcasting. You are comfortable writing a check or giving small amounts.

Major gifts are made from capital assets. It could be stocks, bonds, mutual funds, and/or property. These are transformational gifts that organizations typically allow you to pay over a period of time. When you make the gift over time, it is called a pledge and you are legally bound to fulfill that gift.

---

10 "Private Foundations and Donor-Advised Funds." *Foundation Source*, 2018.

Legacy gifts also can be transformational—both for you and the organization. These also might come from stocks, bonds, mutual funds, and/or property. And, as with major gifts, if made over time, you have made a legally binding pledge to fulfill the gift.

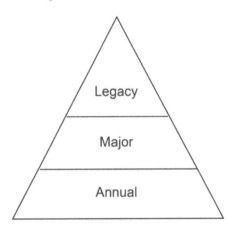

Giving Pyramid

As you become more involved with a charity, you move up the giving pyramid, making more significant gifts. With planning, you can include other types of giving that work for you. As they say, no gift is too small. Working with your advisor can help you determine your individual budget for giving, and if it's right for you, can help structure larger gifts.

In the upcoming chapters, I invite you to read some inspiring stories of people who were able to make gifts they never imagined possible.

CHAPTER 4

DUAL INCOME, NO CHILDREN

Continuing a Legacy of Giving

David Kahn is a man who was proud and honored to follow in his father's footsteps—personally, professionally, and philanthropically. In 2010, when I met David and his wife Beverly, they had just moved from Chicago to Oregon to retire. They were in their early 50s and living the American dream.

David proudly shared the story of his father, Sol, who immigrated to America as a young man. He stepped off the boat with big dreams and $10 in his pocket. When he got into real estate in Chicago, he had found his calling. He built a successful business, married the love of his life, and they had two sons, David and Ben. After they finished college, both sons joined the family business. They learned so much from Sol—how to be successful in real estate, how to prosper in a family-owned business, how to have a happy marriage, and how to give back through philanthropy.

When Sol retired, he left the business to David and Ben, and created a private foundation. The mission of his foundation was to engage inner-city youth to complete high school. Any young person who joined the program and graduated would receive a scholarship for two years of college or trade school. The brothers helped their father with the foundation from the start.

Even after they retired from the business, the brothers went back to Chicago twice a year to assist Sol and the foundation staff in the selection of program participants and to watch those young people graduate.

Over a 20-year period, their foundation made it possible for more than 5,000 inner-city teens to graduate from high school and continue their education—giving each a hand up that could help lead them out of intergenerational poverty.

David shared with me that their work on the foundation had brought him and his brother closer together. David and Beverly had no children of their own, but his brother and wife did. Ben's children were involved in the work of the foundation, just like David and Ben, and they were next in line to keep it going. David couldn't have been more proud of his nieces and nephews and the work they continued to do together.

Inspired and impressed, I asked David, "What about your legacy? What are you going to create?"

He froze.

After a long pause, he said, "I've never thought about that!"

That's when we got to work. He and Beverly had never considered leaving a legacy of their own. They had gotten involved with a number of nonprofits in Portland; their charitable giving and volunteering kept them busy and was a great source of satisfaction to them both. But they had not thought beyond those activities.

I was with the Oregon Community Foundation, and we were one of the nonprofits that David and Beverly had gotten involved with. When they invited me to come out to their home for our next meeting, they took me on a tour of the grounds. Their garden was beautiful and peaceful. We walked along a quaint footpath that cut right through the garden. A young family met us on the path, and Beverly greeted them so warmly I thought they were houseguests or family.

Beverly turned to me and said, "I'd like you to meet our neighbors, Joe, Ellen, and this little guy is Peter."

It turns out that when they moved to this lovely little community, they discovered their neighbors would cut through their yard to get to downtown. Instead of putting up a fence, they created a wonderful garden with a walking path and bench for the community to use. What a great demonstration of their kindness and generosity. And here I was coming to talk with them about their core values and what leaving a legacy could look like for a wealthy couple with no children.

It was no surprise to me when respect, kindness, and opportunity were the core values that surfaced from our discussion. David described how these values were passed down from his father. No matter how successful he was, Sol was always kind and treated everyone with respect.

David was already following in Sol's footsteps in his new community. Like his dad, David loved talking with young people. Every time he'd meet a teen, he'd engage them in conversation, always treating them with kindness and respect. David found that there was a recurring theme in their conversations. The teens complained they had nowhere to go and nothing to do. He also noticed that a lot of them loved to skateboard.

As a real estate expert, David knew that most cities struggle with allowing kids to skateboard because they can cause damage to sidewalks, curbs, planters, and more. He and the kids thought it would be great if they could build a skatepark where they could engage in the sport they love, without ruining the streets and sidewalks of their town. Both David and Beverly became champions of the project. They had just taken their proposal to the city, hoping to get some funding for it. They also talked with local business owners and asked them to donate money as well.

Of course, they also wanted to contribute to the project. In addition, David and Beverly realized that with the right giving tools, they could accomplish even more for the young people in their community once the skatepark was built.

Clearly, they were very familiar with the private foundation model because of Sol's foundation. However, setting up and running a private foundation is a huge undertaking. Rather than administering a foundation, hiring staff, and all that goes with it, David wanted an option that would allow them to focus on giving.

I suggested we create a donor-advised fund, which is like a mini private foundation. You have all of the fun of giving without the administrative hassle. They chose to use the Oregon Community Foundation to be the home of their donor-advised fund. All they had to do was fill out a form and make their donation.

They also could have chosen to set up a donor-advised fund with a national charity or a single nonprofit using a fund agreement. These agreements are typically written in layman's terms, so they are easy to understand. Some organizations have the forms online, making them easy to complete.

Now that we knew how they wanted to give, we were ready to explore their options for funding the donor-advised fund. David met with his accountant to determine which asset was the appropriate one for them to donate. They chose appreciated securities. His cost basis of the securities was $60,000, and they were now worth $100,000.

We set up the donor-advised fund to be wholly expendable, which meant they could grant all the money out of the fund and replenish it whenever they chose. They were not only major advocates for the community skatepark, they were financial contributors, donating about 10% of the total cost of the project.

By making an outright gift of securities to a charitable account, they received a tax deduction for the fair market value of the asset. Since the deduction is limited to 30% of adjusted gross income, they couldn't deduct the full value of the donation. But, it still resulted in a very healthy tax savings for them. The additional deduction has a five-year carry forward for tax purposes until it is used up. In addition to the current tax deduction, David and Beverly will not have to pay capital gains on the $40,000 in appreciation. They also removed those assets from their estate.

You should have seen the look in their eyes the day we finalized everything. As they signed the last document, it all hit home for them. They had just created a mini version of Sol's foundation. They couldn't believe how easy it was, and they loved the resources available from the community foundation.

Best of all for them, this was just the beginning of their charitable giving.

Best of all for me was being able to assist two caring, generous people as they found the tools to become satisfied givers in their own right, changing the world through leadership and philanthropy.

Remember, you do not have to be as wealthy as the Kahn's to create a donor-advised fund.

Personal Reflection

Where do you see need in your community? How could you be a catalyst for change?

_____

_____

_____

_____

_____

_____

_____

_____

_____

_____

Diversify an Asset

I first met Sam and Stacy in 2001, just after they'd relocated from California to retire. This was not their first big move. They had retired in Portland because of the cost of living, quality of life, and lifestyle. "We embrace every new place we move to, and this will be no different. We support local businesses and local charities." They were looking for a new attorney, accountant and financial advisor.

Finding the right advisors was important because Sam had been an executive for a multinational engineering company. Throughout his 25-year career, his compensation included stock options, which allowed him to purchase the stock he owned at a very low price. The company was very successful. As a result, his stocks appreciated over time and were now worth $4.5 million. They knew each state applies different rules towards estates and trusts. Since I was working for a trust company at the time, their attorney referred them to me so that I could help them with their accounts.

It was a joy to work with Stacy. She was warm, welcoming, and radiated positive energy. Sam's success had made it possible for her to live well—beautiful homes in each of the places they'd lived and time to pursue her love of the theatre and the arts (and anything else she might have wanted to do). She managed their personal finances and balanced the checkbook to the penny every month. Even though they had no children, she wanted to make sure their estate and trust arrangements were updated and complied with state law.

Seven years later, in July of 2008, I met Sam and Stacy again. It was delightful to see them. We hugged each other. At this point, I was at the Oregon Community Foundation, and they had been in the Northwest for more than six years. They had established relations with an attorney, accountant and financial advisor. They were thriving on the vibrant lifestyle of Portland; they loved living in the Pearl District. They could walk or bike to everything they enjoyed. They told me about their involvement in a few local theaters and the Oregon Museum of Science and Industry (OMSI).

We caught up on some of the planning they had put in place since we last met. "Remember our nieces and nephews?" they asked.

"Yes, I do," I answered.

"Our advisor gave us an excellent recommendation to create college savings plans for them. Since we last met, we created six 529 plans. We are so thankful for our fortune," they shared, grinning ear to ear. "We want our family to have the advantages education provides."

In college, Stacy had been a theatre major. It was the start of a lifelong passion for the arts. So, it was natural for her to volunteer in the arts community wherever they lived. Portland was no different. She loved using her time to promote the arts, particularly small performing arts centers. "I love the arts," Stacy told me. Finding emerging playwrights was also a passion for her. "Supporting the creativity of a mind is magnificent. I want to encourage magnificence," she stated emphatically.

"I am here for you. What questions do you have?" I asked.

"How do we organize our giving?" they asked. "When we're gone, we want whatever's left to go to the community. Our attorney sent us here to get assistance," Stacy added.

"What are the values you want to pass down?" I asked them.

"Community," said Sam. "Every time we've moved, we ... well, really, Stacy has become deeply involved in the local community."

"Opportunity," added Stacy. "We want to create opportunities for others," they nodded together.

"Tell me about your current giving," I said. "A few minutes ago, you mentioned some small community theatres and OMSI. What else are you doing?"

They told me they attended other charitable events—mostly fundraisers their friends were involved in. They made small donations in cash, wrote checks, and they put some donations on credit cards. Their larger gifts were made with appreciated stock. (It was good to know they still had appreciated stock.). Stacy thought that it was all pretty haphazard and could be a lot more organized, perhaps more strategic.

I had a few options to share with them:

1. Current giving
2. Split-interest giving
3. Bequest giving.

Then, I addressed their desire to organize their giving and be more strategic.

Current Giving

In order to organize current giving, I recommended they create a donor-advised fund. By doing this, they could achieve a number of things. First, they could donate the appreciated stock to the community foundation to fund it. They'd get an immediate deduction of the current value of the stock and wouldn't have to pay capital gains. Second, because it is donor-advised, they could choose where each donation goes—in this case, OMSI and Stacy's favorite theatres.

By using a donor-advised fund, they receive a full accounting of the grants made to the nonprofits at the end of each year. They give where they choose. Also, the donations made to the fund during the year are organized and can be turned over to their accountant when it is time to prepare their taxes.

They really liked this option. Their giving was going to be limited to a few organizations—OMSI and the theaters. OMSI had solid financials, a strong board, and lots of community involvement. This made them feel very confident that the money would be used wisely and for the express purpose they were supporting. An outright gift to OMSI seemed like an excellent choice.

But the theaters were not as robust organizationally or financially. This raised some very valid concerns. Would annually giving a large amount of money to such small organizations cause more harm than good? Would they know how to invest it? We would have to look more closely at each theatre group and see what would make sense.

After researching the financials of the theatres, they were not comfortable making a large outright gift to any of them. I showed them how a donor-advised fund could be set up to allow them to leave a letter of instruction for ongoing grants. For example, they could stipulate that the annual distribution be divided, 50% to OMSI, 25% to one of the theatres, and 25% to the other theatre—or any funding distribution they choose. This is called endowing your fund. You may also see it called a legacy fund or directed fund.

Sam and Stacy created a donor-advised fund to consolidate their giving. Each year they would put in $20K, and then grant it to OMSI and the theatres in amounts that made sense for each organization. The fund was set up so they could change recommended grants from the fund each year. They decided to wait before providing the letter of instruction.

Split-Interest Gift

A split-interest gift was also discussed. These can be made two different ways.

The first is a charitable gift annuity. Because of their ages (Sam and Stacy were 68 and 69 respectively), annuity rates, as determined by the American Council on Gift Annuities, were going to be less than 5%. That did not provide an adequate income stream for them. Had they been older, this would have been a more viable option for them because the payout rate would be higher. They declined this option.

The second method is a charitable remainder trust. They were already making gifts of appreciated stock. Doing so in a charitable remainder trust could provide many benefits to them. With a trust, you choose the payout rate and the trustee. You defer capital gains and get a tax deduction. By diversifying your investments in the trust, you can increase your income. After you die, the remainder of the money in the trust goes to the charities you chose to benefit when you created it.

We ran the numbers, and they were happily surprised. We looked at a charitable remainder trust for the rest of both of their lives with a payout rate of 6%. If it were funded with $1,000,000 of stock, it would provide an annual income stream of $60,000 and a partial income tax deduction the first year. The stock would be sold and diversified in the trust. This diversification may appreciate in value and keep pace with inflation. After they died, the balance or remainder would go to their favorite charities. This can be set up so your financial advisor manages the trust, or the charity can.

They wanted to think about this option a little more deeply and talk it over with their financial advisor. A week later they called to inform me that their financial advisor thought the charitable remainder trust was an excellent way to diversify the stock and to reduce and defer taxes. Their attorney drafted the document creating the trust, and Sam and Stacy funded it.

Bequest Giving

After an in-depth conversation, Sam and Stacy decided they wanted the remainder of their estate to go to the Oregon Community Foundation. Fortunately, we had some time to thoughtfully work on what that part of the plan would look like.

This is an excellent example of how an individual or family can diversify an asset. In Sam and Stacy's case, it was corporate stock, but it can also be another asset like a business interest or property.

Personal Reflection

Consider your values. What is important to you? How do you want to make an impact in this area? What do you want your life to stand for?

_____

_____

_____

_____

_____

_____

_____

Anything is Possible

Jane and James were referrals from an attorney. I first met them in 2010, when they wanted to learn about community foundations. After college, they had become successful beyond their wildest dreams. At 57 and 60, they had already accomplished more than they ever imagined possible. Jane and James were the first in their families to go to college. They met in the college of business at the University of Alaska where they were both in the marketing club. They fell in love while working on a project together.

They were true entrepreneurs and made it big in the advertising business. Now, they were worth $40 million. They owned property around the world as well as cars and planes. They had it all.

They were delightful people, and grateful for all they had achieved. They were just beginning to update their estate plan, and their attorney had sent them to me for an education on the various ways to give. They had some relatives, but no children. They wanted to leave the majority of their assets to charity.

They had no idea where to begin to give to their family.

"How much are they prepared to receive?" I asked. In unison, without missing a beat, they replied, "Nothing!" The family had no idea of their success. They wanted to leave something to each person in the family, but not so much that they couldn't handle the wealth. "We want to make their life easier, but we don't want to turn them into people that they're not," they stated.

This was something they had been discussing with their attorney, and they were still considering their options.

I asked them to tell me about their family members.

The family lived in Alaska. Jane told me about her 10 relatives—brothers, sisters, nieces, and nephews. Two were attending community college. James told me about his 10 relatives—aunts, uncles, and cousins. No college educations on his side either.

"What do you want to accomplish with a gift to them?" I asked. That was a good thing for them to think about.

Next, I provided a few alternatives to put context around what helping a family member might look like:

1.   Leave an outright gift to family
2.   Leave it all to charity
3.   Use a split-interest gift that would accomplish both

They left with charitable ideas to think about. I touched base with their attorney, and he thanked me for educating them. Because their estate was so big, and their business was booming, they put the charitable piece to the back of their mind for a while.

Periodically, they would meet with their attorney. Six years later, they finally got to the place where they were ready to discuss the estate and charitable plan. At this point, they were worth $60 million. Jane and James were ready to express their gratitude by creating a philanthropic plan.

Since the start of their marriage and their business, they had been equal owners. Choosing where their money would go would also be an equal decision.

As we continued our conversation, it was clear that providing for family members was important, and so was leaving donations to their alma mater, environmental causes, and women's healthcare organizations.

We discussed the gifts to family and what that would look like. Should they leave outright gifts to their family?

None of the family lived in the financial domain they had created. Family members had no idea about their success and had no experience managing large amounts of money. They were good, hardworking people but really had no financial acumen. They couldn't imagine any of their family receiving an outright gift. They were concerned it might be squandered. Giving a large inheritance was off the table.

Leave It All to Charity

They were comfortable giving directly to the organizations they supported. They were already philanthropic, but it did not accomplish their goal to help family. A split-interest gift was an interesting option to explore.

Based on their net worth, 20 relatives (who were not financially savvy) could receive an annual inheritance between $25,000 and $250,000 per year.

"You're kidding me," they said. "That is a wide range."

"Of course it is, but you choose. There are a few ways we can accomplish this. It's your choice. What would be an appropriate amount of money for them to receive?"

We discussed the options.

A gift annuity would provide an income stream for life to the family member, and anything that remained upon their death would go to charity. The annuity is based on the fiscal strength of the charity and would have different payout rates to different family members because it is based on their ages. Jane and James didn't like the fact that family members would receive different amounts of money. This option was declined.

Next, we discussed charitable trusts. Charitable trusts provide an income stream for life, or 20 years, or both. They wanted things to be equal and not burdensome. The trust is a separate entity, and Jane and James would determine who receives the payout, for how long, and the specific payout rate. That meant they could guarantee every family member would be treated equally.

They loved that idea. It meant they could create charitable trusts that would provide each family member the same amount of money for the same amount of time. Twenty separate charitable trusts would accomplish their gift goals. They chose a payout of 20 years, with anything remaining after that going to charity.

Jane and James brought this information to the attorney, so he could finish drafting the estate plan. They finally had some peace of mind.

The estate plan included two specific bequests—women's healthcare and the University of Alaska. Upon their death, $40 million would be used to create 20 charitable trusts. There would be one trust created for each family member, with a 6% payout over 20 years. The 6% annual payout rate would provide $120,000 per year for 20 years. If one of the family members died or was no longer living at the time of Jane and James' death, that share of the trust would go to charity.

They felt really good helping family.

Creating the charitable trusts would use only $40 million of the $60 million, so they had to consider what to do with the other $20 million. Where did they want to make a difference? There was still more work to do.

They decided to have the $20 million go directly to charity or a legacy fund.

We looked at the $20 million. Who did they want to help? Education played a key role in their lives. They had met at college. Without their business degrees, they believed they would never have been so successful. They chose to give $2 million to endow a dean's chair at the school of business at the University of Alaska. Another $2 million would go to organizations that provide women's healthcare. That totaled $4 million.

This left $16 million for scholarships. They also wanted to help students—students like them who were the first in their family to go to college. They created scholarships that helped Oregonians who wanted to study business and needed financial aid. This scholarship fund would be administered by OCF. Oregon is one of two states in the country that has a statewide scholarship clearinghouse. This means students can apply to one source for multiple scholarships. Even though OCF administers the scholarship fund, family members may participate on the review panel in a minority capacity.

The calculations were made to zero out estate taxes upon their death. By using a charitable remainder trust, Jane and James were able to provide an income stream to family members and leave gifts to charity. To recap, upon death, a $2 million bequest will be made to the University of Alaska to endow a dean's chair position. Another $2 million will go to women's healthcare. The remaining $16 million will go to scholarship funds for those with financial need who are the first of their family to go to college.

Another happy story of giving that provides opportunities for others to excel!

Jane and James Estate Plan

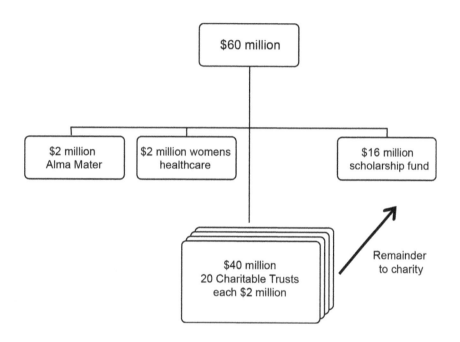

Personal Reflection

Would you like others involved in deciding where to give charitable dollars? To help you decide where to give, you can include family, friends, community, nonprofit organizations, and/or others.

_____

_____

_____

_____

_____

CHAPTER 5

BUSINESS OWNERS

You've made it! Can you imagine running a family-owned business for more than 30 years? Then, imagine further that your father started the business with a modest family farm and a produce stand by the side of the road that grew into three prosperous suburban grocery stores. When you come back from college, your dad makes you a partner, and when he retires, it becomes your business. You work long hours, make a good living, and raise a family. One day, a major corporation makes an offer to buy the business. You say yes and become a multimillionaire. That's exactly what happened to Joel and Marcia Westcott.

Structuring Your Giving

Their lawyer referred them to me because they didn't know what they were going to do with all that money. Until then, Joel and Marcia had lived well but fairly simply. They still lived in the first home they ever purchased, making only some modest upgrades over the years. Marcia was active in the community, volunteering at the local library, which was across the street from their first store and around the corner from their house.

Joel started working on the family farm when he was just six years old, selling produce from a stand at the side of the road. By the time he was ten, his dad gave him full charge of the stand. The popularity of the farm stand grew every year under Joel's management; so much so, that the family decided to open a grocery store. It became the first of three the family would own. As the business continued to grow, Joel's dad made the decision to join an association of individually owned groceries. This enabled them to maximize their purchasing power and lower their overall costs.

All through high school, Joel divided his time between school and working—either on the farm or in one of the stores, alongside other kids from the neighborhood who worked there after school and on weekends. When he went off to college, he worked at the grocery stores during the summers, wherever he was needed.

After Joel graduated, he married Marcia, his childhood sweetheart, and his dad brought him into the business. Under their joint leadership, the business continued to thrive and support not only their own families, but the families of their 30 full-time employees as well. Over the years, hundreds of kids from the neighborhoods around the stores worked part-time jobs after school and during the summers to earn money for their first car or to add to their college funds.

In addition to working hard, Joel's dad believed in giving back to the community that supported their business. His father always gave anonymously. Joel and Marcia had carried on that tradition after his father retired. Joel shared with me, "My dad always used to say, 'The project is what's important.' I'm just grateful I can carry on his good work. Like him, I don't need recognition or to have a building named after me. There's nothing wrong with that, it's just not our style."

The family supported the local library, where Marcia volunteered, the parks and recreation foundation, and Little League teams. In addition to giving to local charities, Joel's father made sure that his employees' children would have the same educational opportunities that Joel had by giving them college scholarships. The family never considered that what they were doing was philanthropy; they just thought of giving as a way of thanking everyone who helped them along the way.

Joel had worked hard from the age of six through his adult life. He loved what he did, but he had one regret. He had always longed to be that kid on the soccer field. There just was never time for him to participate in sports. But, after his father had retired and Joel was running the stores, he began supporting elementary school, middle school, and high school soccer groups who came in to ask him to sponsor their teams.

He was both flattered and excited. He bought the jerseys. He purchased ads at the sports fields. He helped them buy their equipment. Like his dad, Joel also gave to the local parks and recreation sports programs. Though he was never able to realize his dream of playing soccer, he made that dream come true for many kids in his community, including his own son.

Joel was delighted that he could give his son Michael a different life than the one he had. After school, Michael would often go to the store to help Joel. Sometimes, he would go to the library across the street from the store where his mom volunteered to read or do homework. But, they made sure he had time to do other things—Michael did join a soccer team and he loved it. When he was named team captain in high school, Joel and Marcia were bursting with pride.

Michael went to college at Joel's alma mater, Oregon State University, to study agriculture. His family had sold the farm that Joel grew up on many years earlier. But, Michael loved rural life and moved to eastern Oregon after graduating where he became a farmer—just like his grandfather.

After more than 30 years in the grocery business, Joel and Marcia got an offer they couldn't refuse. As a result, they sold their three stores to a major corporation and walked away with millions. They never could have imagined the good fortune they would receive, and now they could retire. Another American dream comes true.

Larger Donations

I first sat down with Joel and Marcia in the summer of 2010. Their son, Michael, was set for life at this point. Joel and Marcia had a general idea of what they wanted to do with their money. Their community was important to them—they saw how their practice of giving throughout their working lives had already made a difference for the kids and the teams they supported. The library foundation was important to them, too—kids had to learn how to read to get ahead. But, they'd never made a gift larger than $5,000 before. Most of their giving was a few hundred dollars, here and there. That day, they wanted to learn how to make a bigger impact in their community. Creating a plan for their legacy was new territory.

They wanted to preserve the family tradition of giving locally. They wanted to stay true to the values they'd learned from watching Joel's dad give back, year after year. They wanted to make significant gifts that could become the catalyst for positive changes. At the same time, they were humble and proud that they could be the vessel to do this. It gave me goose bumps.

One of the concerns Joel and Marcia had was how they could continue to give to the library and the soccer teams. Libraries and parks are government entities, which can receive donations. However, unless that organization has a separate nonprofit to accept large sums of money, there is always the concern that the money might not be spent the way the donor wants it to be.

Even though they had so much money to give, committing to a big gift was intimidating. We took baby steps and started out small so they could learn to be thoughtful givers. We began by reviewing all of their past charitable giving. Their accountant provided the details. They decided to continue giving to the groups they had consistently supported. They would make annual donations, ranging in size from $500 – $5,000, to the library and to the children's soccer program (through the local parks and recreation foundation).

But, they also wanted to do something more for the library. They wanted to make a large donation—more than they had ever given before—and they wanted their gift to remain anonymous. Though the bulk of their giving would be local, they decided to also make charitable gifts in eastern Oregon, where Michael lived.

Joel and Marcia had a couple of options:

1) Create a donor-advised fund
2) Create a legacy or donor-directed fund

They chose to begin with a donor-advised fund, which was created with a gift of appreciated stock in the amount of $50,000. This would be a wholly expendable fund, during their lifetime, to help them get acquainted with how donor-advised funds work. This fund provided them flexibility to add new organizations each year. They could recommend grants and zero out the fund balance if they chose to. And, they could add more money at any time, then once again grant out all the money to their charities. One element they really liked was that the donor-advised fund allowed them to give anonymously. Michael joined us for our next meeting to help create the fund that would support causes in his community in eastern Oregon.

Over the next five years, Joel and Marcia became more comfortable with using their donor-advised fund to give to the soccer program and the library. They were not only comfortable—they were having a blast. They loved how easy it was to give anonymously.

Now, they were ready to step up to the next level. I introduced them to the concept of a directed fund. A directed (legacy) fund is a permanent fund that annually distributes a percentage to the specific nonprofits you choose. The percentage is typically about 5%. The calculation is based on a three- or five-year rolling average of the fund's assets. The formula mitigates any highs and lows in market fluctuation.

What this meant is that they could leave the remainder of their estate to the directed fund and be assured that the library and soccer program would receive money every year in perpetuity. They loved the idea, but then a scowl crossed Joel's face and he asked, "What if the library or soccer team ceases to exist?"

It was the right question to ask. I was able to tell them that the great thing about a directed fund is that you can place qualifications on the gift. I explained that if the library or park ceased to exist, we could put in contingent instructions.

Marcia's passion for reading was the primary reason she volunteered all those years at the library. If that library ever closed, she wanted to find a way to continue to support libraries and a love of reading. We did some research and found an Oregon organization called SMART (Start Making A Reader Today).

SMART is a successful statewide program that provides low-income kids with reading support and access to books. The program involves volunteers to help kids learn to read, and supports the libraries that implement the programs goals. The SMART program met all of Marcia's criteria and served children in eastern Oregon, where Michael lived. If her library was closed down, SMART would be the recipient of those funds, and they would continue to support access to reading around the state.

Joel and Marcia's story is an example of how a donor-advised fund can be used to provide anonymous gifts at a level far beyond the donors' imagination. They engaged their son in the process and made it possible for him to also give in his community by setting up a separate donor-advised fund that he administered on his own.

The directed fund was a powerful tool that established their ongoing legacy. This instrument gave them the flexibility to define alternative options and continue to provide support in the community if the library could no longer operate. They loved having that option.

Personal Reflection

What would you do with the money if you suddenly found yourself richer than you ever dreamed possible? Do you need to wait for that day to come, or could you begin giving now?

_____

_____

_____

_____

_____

CHAPTER 6

SINGLE

No Heirs

Alex Johansson, 58 years old and never married, showed up in my office while I was working for a trust company. He was an only child, and his parents were also only children. He had a great job and an inheritance of $1.5 million to manage. Alex believed he was extremely fortunate.

Now, to some of you, $1.5 million might seem like fabulous wealth. To others, it's nice but no big deal. However, when you live as modestly as Alex did, that money seemed like a fortune. And, to a man like Alex, it represented an amazing opportunity to create a legacy, to do good in the world. Alex and I worked together to help him do that.

He was an unassuming man with slightly gray hair, a scruffy beard and mustache, and a warm and friendly face. If his hair and beard were all white, he would look just like Santa. He was born and raised in Portland, Oregon, and most recently had been living in Alaska.

Alex had a concrete plan for growing that million and a half dollars to be about four or five million dollars by the time he passed. But, why would a guy with nobody to give it to even care? A lot of people would tell him, "Spend it!" But Alex wanted to leave a legacy.

As he told me about himself, I learned he had an unhurried and thoughtful approach to life. "My parents and grandparents lived frugally. They were good people," Alex recalled. "I admired them so much. They worked hard; they saved their money."

His paternal grandparents immigrated to the United States from Sweden with nothing but the clothes on their backs and a few dollars in their pockets. They came to America looking for a better life. But the life they'd envisioned didn't exist. There were no streets paved with gold. Rather, they had to make their own way. His grandfather became a plumber and built a successful business. They embraced the challenges along with the opportunities and succeeded in making this country their home and giving their family a wonderful life.

They were able to afford to send their son, Alex's dad, to college and medical school. While completing his internship, he met and fell in love with Alex's mom, who was also completing her internship. Back then, very few women went to medical school or became doctors. She was a pioneer in her profession. After completing their training, Alex's parents opened a general practice in the town where they lived. Their friends and neighbors became their patients. They even made house calls.

Alex's career was in government service. He worked for the Social Security Administration. He made a good living and had a solid retirement benefit accrued from his years of service. With no kids and no family to raise, he was able to live very comfortably.

Some people say that government employees are not helpful and rather slow. Alex was the exact opposite. You see, Alex made it his mission in life to do his job by the rules and to use those rules to help people. For example, one couple that had lived together for more than 50 years came to see him. The man gently pushed her wheelchair into place in front of Alex's desk. They had children and grandchildren together, but they had never been legally married. They were embarrassed about it and were afraid that now that they needed social security benefits, they might not be able to qualify.

When Alex traced their history, he discovered that they had lived together long enough to be recognized as being in a common-law marriage in their state— legally, they were considered married. He reassured them that they would get the Social Security benefits they had paid for all their working lives. He helped them get the paperwork done.

As they worked on the application, Alex learned that she was in the wheelchair because they could not afford hip replacement surgery for her. She had not walked in 15 years. With Alex's help, they would also be able to get Medicare, and the money they needed to live on, now that they could no longer work.

This is just one example of the ways he helped people every day he came to work. He gave people hope, as he made sure they got the benefits they earned and deserved. This was my new client. We would work together to create his legacy—a legacy that would continue to do good in the world and honor his family long after he was gone.

The challenge was that Alex wasn't sure what would be the best use of his money. When you're an individual who is unsure of how you want to create or manage a legacy, there are three primary issues to consider:

1) What is the legacy I want to leave?
2) Can I simplify my giving?
3) Who will help me if I become incapacitated or terminally ill?

Choosing Your Legacy

When thinking about the type of legacy you want to leave, you need to consider what's important to you and why. For these kinds of conversations, I always like to start by talking to my clients about their values—what is most important to them and/or what was most important to the loved ones they want to honor.

Scholarship Funds

During our discussion, Alex shared that his parents had a deep love for music. As a child, they had encouraged Alex to take violin lessons, and he had played the violin with his local symphony orchestra.

In Alaska, Alex volunteered in the neighborhood middle school by providing violin lessons to deserving students. He also brought violins into the school for the students who couldn't afford to rent or buy them. He had been doing this for the past 11 years. He truly enjoyed the time spent volunteering at the school and planned to continue this project for as long as he was physically able to do it.

His lifelong love of music, a passion instilled in him by his parents, became one aspect of his giving plan. Alex decided that he would like to use a portion of his money to help children learn to make music and give them opportunities to be exposed to great music.

With so many schools cutting music programs, he realized that, after he was gone, his legacy fund could further the work he was doing and more. Alex realized he could ensure that children with talent could get an opportunity to pursue music.

Throughout our conversation, the importance of Alex's family and their influence on him also became evident. So, the other component of his giving plan was going to honor his parents and grandparents. He decided to establish two separate scholarship funds.

For his parents, he decided to provide scholarships for promising students who might not be able to afford medical school. Because his mother had become a doctor when so few women could, Alex decided to prioritize scholarships specifically for first generation women who wanted to attend medical school.

For his grandparents, Alex wanted to honor the bravery it took to move to a new country and start a new life. If his grandfather hadn't built such a successful plumbing business, his father would never have been able to go to medical school. That first generation boldness was something he admired and wanted to share with others.

There are many ways to create scholarship funds. Alex and I discussed the following possibilities:

1) Working directly with a college or university
2) Creating a trust and designating an administrator who identifies scholarship recipients (regardless of the school they choose to attend)

3) Working with a private or public foundation that acts as a clearinghouse for scholarships and manages the giving process

Deciding which of these possibilities best suits your needs takes some consideration and depends upon your particular situation. If you decide to establish a scholarship at a specific college or university, then you will typically work directly with that school to coordinate the details.

Setting up a trust with a designated administrator presents different options based on where you live and how much you would like to invest in the fund. To that end, you will likely need to do some homework to explore your options. Funds established with foundations are typically coordinated by a staff of employees who manage and administer scholarships for a variety of groups.

For Alex, our decision was simplified a little. He planned to live in Oregon after he retired and wanted his scholarships to benefit students in that area. Oregon is one of two states in the nation (Vermont is the other) that has statewide scholarship programs.

The Oregon Office of Student Access and Completion (OSAC) is a state agency that operates as a clearinghouse for scholarships. OSAC not only administers their own scholarship, but they also process scholarships for the Oregon Community Foundation (OCF), US Bank, private companies and family foundations. This partnership allows students to complete one application and then apply for up to 20 different scholarships. Alex ultimately chose to set his fund up at the OCF so all students in Oregon would have access to his scholarships.

Simplify Giving

Alex confessed, "My giving isn't that much, but I want to keep some flexibility in my estate plans in case things change." With this in mind, we made sure that his fund could be modified at any time during his lifetime.

He also wanted to simplify his giving. At this time, one of Alex's donations involved buying musical instruments and personally delivering them to schools. This was time consuming and occasionally difficult because some of the instruments were too big for his car. Alex had also tried giving anonymously, but that hadn't work for him.

I provided him with a number of options that would both fulfill and simplify his goals. They included ways to manage his giving both during his life and through his estate. After reflection and discussion, Alex decided on the following approach:

1) Create a donor-advised fund at the OCF to simplify his current giving. He would set up the fund by donating stock that had appreciated in value, which would allow him to give anonymously. And, he would receive an immediate tax deduction on that donation. Implemented.

2) Create three legacy funds that would be drafted, but only funded upon Alex's death. Implemented.

   a) Honor parents—A legacy fund to provide scholarship assistance to medical school for women who were also first-generation Americans. He named the fund after his parents.

   b) Honor grandparents—Named after his grandparents, this legacy fund would give scholarships to students to attend schools that taught the trades.

   c) Promote music appreciation and music education—This legacy fund would purchase violins for promising youth and fund middle school music programs.

Help If You Become Incapacitated or Terminally Ill

Planning for every eventuality is important, so Alex and I discussed his legal and financial options if he were to become incapacitated or terminally ill.

Since Alex had a significant estate and no family or friends to count on when he returned to Oregon, we focused on traditional options.

I explained that he could retain a fiduciary—a trustee who could act on his behalf and manage his funds. I gave Alex a list of possible corporate and individual trustees who provide these services so he could contact them and learn about their offerings. The list included corporate bank trustees, regional and local trustees, and individual trustees. Each option had pros and cons.

After narrowing the list down, Alex took time to meet the fiduciaries he was interested in working with to discuss the details of his situation. He ended up selecting a regional trust company that also had trust powers in Alaska, where he still lived.

Your life might not look like Alex's. But, whatever your situation, it's worth considering not only what you want to leave as a lasting legacy, but also how you're going to do it. The best way to do this is to meet with people like me (or your financial and legal advisors) who can help you look at your unique situation and work with you to create a lasting legacy.

Personal Reflection

What outcomes would you like to have in the world? In your community?

_____

_____

_____

_____

_____

_____

_____

_____

_____

_____

Life Insurance as an Investment

Laura came to see me three years after her mother had died. Her insurance advisor had referred her to me. Laura was in her early 40s, single with no children, and had just inherited $800,000. The inheritance had come as a complete surprise to her. Laura's father had died of a heart attack when she was very young. Before passing, he had purchased a life insurance policy that listed her mother as the beneficiary.

As a result, Laura and her mom had enough money to live modestly without ever touching the principal and without her mom ever having to work. What a gift! His foresight and planning took care of both his beloved wife and child. Laura's mother invested the money wisely. While Laura knew there had been an insurance benefit, she never knew exact dollar amounts.

Laura's mother worked with a financial advisor to invest the insurance proceeds. The advisor educated her and provided the emotional and financial tools she needed to become self-sufficient. Her mother learned to budget and created a spending plan. Then, she stuck to the plan, no matter what. Her plan included keeping a reserve to help her establish credit. As a result, she never had to get a job.

When I met her, Laura was working as a barista in a neighborhood coffee shop. She lived off her modest salary and used some of the investment income from her inheritance to supplement her income and treat herself. She loved working in the coffee shop. She felt at home there and knew all the customers and their favorite coffee drinks. She had no ambitions for a bigger job or a new career.

Honestly, $800,000 was more money than she'd ever imagined having. In fact, she and her mother had always lived so frugally that, when her mother received her cancer diagnosis, Laura wondered if she'd be able to pay for the funeral. She told me, "I feel like I won the saddest lottery in the world." The look on her face said it all.

Like so many people who inherit money, Laura would much rather have her loved one alive than have the money. During the three years since her mother's passing, she had very mixed feelings about whether or not to spend the money. When she bought a few things with some of the money, nothing big, she felt guilty. Other times, she looked at her bank balance and felt like she'd won the lottery but couldn't enjoy any of it. Inheriting money felt bittersweet. As Laura shared the story of her mother, tears ran down her cheeks. Her grief was still very raw.

Inheritance, Finances, and Giving

Laura told me she wasn't interested in getting married. She was pretty certain she'd be single for the rest of her life, and she was at peace with that. She had come to me because she had a few big concerns she didn't know how to handle on her own. First, she wanted to create a plan to live off this money responsibly, just as she and her mom had done. She would need to work with her financial advisor to do that.

Planning early was a family tradition. Her father had certainly planned ahead by buying that insurance policy. Her mother had planned ahead by working with her financial advisor as soon as she received the insurance benefit. She had created a diversified portfolio so she could ultimately live off the earnings, support her daughter, and have a comfortable, if modest, life.

With her mom gone and no other relatives, Laura thought she would need someone to settle her affairs after she passed. She was her mom's personal representative, but who would be hers? Laura had aunts, uncles, and cousins. She loved them, but they weren't close. She really was on her own. Her visit with me took on some urgency because she was looking ahead. She wanted to be prepared for whatever came. You see, her father was in his early 40' when he suffered his fatal heart attack—the same age Laura was when I met her.

She wanted to know if the Oregon Community Foundation could serve as her personal representative. That was a simple question to answer. Community foundations do not act as personal representatives or trustees. I suggested that she reach out to a family member, a trusted friend, or a bank or trust company to fulfill that role.

She also wanted to honor her mother. Laura described her mom as "the best role model a girl could have. My mother was smart and beautiful. She always cheered me on and encouraged me to pursue anything I wanted to do. She had this unshakable confidence that I would succeed no matter how challenging the situation was. I know how lucky I was to have her in my life."

Even though she and her mother lived modestly, her mother was generous and helped those in need in their community. Her motto was "live local, give local." Laura wanted to carry on that tradition, which was where the Oregon Community Foundation could help her.

I suggested she create a donor-advised fund. This would allow her to consolidate her giving. If she used the fund to do all of her charitable giving, the Community Foundation would send her a single annual report that detailed and tracked how much she gave and where she gave. This would help her identify her giving patterns and allow her to make giving adjustments at any time.

Selecting a title for the fund was difficult. Laura's initial thoughts were to put her name on it, make up a name that reflected her giving mission, or simply assign it a number. She was uncomfortable putting her name on the fund. She could never shake the feeling that the money wasn't hers. She would gladly give it all back to see her mother again. The random number seemed too impersonal. I suggested that she name the fund after her mother, and Laura's eyes lit up and a brilliant smile crossed her face. They even had different last names; she could maintain her anonymity. With that, the fund was named in honor of her extraordinary mother.

Laura left our final meeting with a sense of joy and relief. She had accomplished a few of the items on her list. She had created a donor-advised fund to honor her mother, and, in doing so, was starting to feel good about inheriting the money. She now had confidence she would use her money wisely and, when she was gone, it would go to the causes she and her mother had cared about.

She needed to do more research on whether a trustee or personal representative would help settle her estate, but our talks had empowered her to investigate her options.

In Laura's situation, we used her donor-advised fund to accomplish a few things. It was a way for her to honor her mother. It consolidated her giving so she could more easily track and follow her donations. It provided a tax deduction because it took that money out of her estate for tax purposes.

Laura is another happy giver who found a way to honor her mother.

Personal Reflection

Identify two or three people (they could be family members, other people you know, or historic figures) who have had a strong influence on you. What values did they transmit to you?

_____

_____

_____

_____

_____

CHAPTER 7

WIDOWS

Legacy Planning

Ruth Allen was a retired pediatric nurse in her late 70s. Widowed when she was in her early 30s, Ruth never had children and never remarried. She was from a wealthy family. Her brothers and sister, nieces and nephews were all well off. But when her mother had died about ten years earlier, there was a big fight over the estate. Ruth hadn't spoken to anyone in her family since. She had invested in rental properties over the years and done quite well. She estimated her net worth to be about $3 million.

For Ruth, nursing wasn't just a job. It was a vocation. Throughout her career, she had traveled the world with nonprofit health organizations donating her time wherever she was needed. When she had time off, she would visit zoos or wild animal parks. She even went on a few safaris.

One year while volunteering in Africa, she met a young man who had created an animal reserve. His passion was infectious. She was so inspired by his commitment to protecting animals and the environment that she gave him a $10,000 donation. It was the largest gift Ruth had ever given to a nonprofit, and it led to a transformational realization. She had found her defining passion—protecting animals and animal habitats. Ruth said, "I like people, but I *love* animals. They don't talk back."

Ruth came to see me with several concerns. She had no one to help settle her affairs or follow her instructions if she became incapacitated. She wanted to increase her income stream. She had grown tired of being a landlord. And, most importantly, she wanted to make a difference for animals and animal habitats in the Pacific Northwest where she lived.

Fiduciary

Like many widows, Ruth didn't have someone to trust and rely on to help her with her affairs if she became ill. I recommended that she consider hiring a fiduciary. A fiduciary is a person who acts on behalf of another person or persons to manage assets. Essentially, a fiduciary is a person or organization that owes to another the duties of good faith and trust. The highest legal duty of one party to another, it also involves being bound ethically to act in the other's best interests.

This person or organization can act as a trustee. A trustee is a person or entity that has a fiduciary duty to another person or entity, called the beneficiary. The trustee holds cash, assets, or a title to property for the benefit of the beneficiary. The trustee's job is to manage the assets in the trust appropriately and to ensure that they are disbursed in the best interests of the beneficiary.

In a broader sense, a fiduciary is a person or entity responsible for acting in the best interests of others—typically an investment client, a company's shareholders, or a beneficiary.

We then discussed the pros and cons between designating a corporate trustee versus an individual trustee, perhaps a good friend or family member. After our conversation, she felt like she had enough information to interview fiduciaries—both independent and corporate.

With guidance from her attorney and accountant, she began to bring together a fiduciary team to represent her interests. That team would act as instructed should she become incapacitated or die.

Charitable Remainder Trust

To address Ruth's need for income, we discussed her portfolio in detail. She owned a lot of appreciated real estate. Since she was tired of being a landlord, I asked her if she would be interested in using her real estate to make a charitable gift. This would increase her income and ultimately support her passion to care for animals and their habitats. I then explained how she could use a charitable remainder trust to accomplish both of these goals and give her a healthy tax write-off.

For many people like Ruth, real estate investments represent the largest portion of their net worth. The question then becomes how to best convert real estate into a higher income-producing asset. A charitable remainder trust is an effective strategy because it gives you two options. You can either pay out the net income generated by the property or sell the property and pay a percentage of the charitable remainder trust's value. If the property is sold, the charitable remainder trust can then reinvest the proceeds into a diversified portfolio. Typical trust payouts are five to seven percent. This also defers capital gains taxes.

Ruth loved the idea. She went ahead and had her attorney draft the documents to create a charitable remainder trust so she could donate her real estate. The trust also helped Ruth take care of her other concerns by identifying a trustee, a beneficiary, and a charity (or charities) that would receive the money when the current beneficiary died (known as the remainder beneficiary).

Ruth was a very savvy investor. She knew her properties inside and out and believed she could best handle the sale. She made herself the initial trustee. Language in the document named successor trustees who would take over after the sale of the property and beyond. Ruth didn't want to deal with administering the trust.

Ruth placed about $1million of her real estate holdings into the trust. It was what we call an irrevocable gift. By doing this, she received an immediate tax deduction. The property was placed into the trust before any sale of the property was agreed upon. As the initial trustee, Ruth would handle the sale of the properties on behalf of the trust. After the rental properties were sold, the trust received the proceeds from the sale. The cash was invested in a diversified portfolio. For the rest of her life, Ruth would receive a five percent payout annually from the trust. When Ruth dies, all assets flow to a legacy fund.

Legacy Fund

Now, it was time for the fun. I helped Ruth create what's called a directed or legacy fund. Since Ruth said she wanted to focus on making a difference for animals and animal habitats in the Pacific Northwest, she quickly pulled together a list of 20 animal and environmental organizations in the area. It was a veritable giving spree. The list included organizations like SOLVE, Friends of the Tualatin River National Wildlife Refuge, and Friends of the Columbia Gorge. Some of the groups were well established, and others were small, fledgling organizations.

We started by discussing the pros and cons of giving outright donations to organizations versus consolidating her giving into the legacy fund. If she gave the money outright to a small organization with little experience handling large gifts, there was the possibility they might not have the internal financial structure and capabilities to manage the gift. The desire to do good work doesn't always include the skills to manage money. Ruth realized that the smaller organizations she was targeting would benefit from the professional money management skills provided by a legacy fund. To cover all scenarios, we included a provision for the money in the event one of the beneficiary organizations closed down. If an organization ceased to exist, the money would be divided equally among the remaining organizations.

I wanted Ruth to see the impact her legacy fund would have on the organizations the fund would support, so I created a great spreadsheet that showed the yearly payout each organization would receive. She had named 20 nonprofits for her fund. If the legacy fund had a corpus of $3 million and paid out 5% per year, or about $150,000, then each organization would receive $7,500 per year in perpetuity.

After looking over the spreadsheet, Ruth unexpectedly asked me if I thought the North Coast Land Conservancy was a worthy organization. I assured her that it was based on due diligence. She then wanted to know what the difference would be if she added them to the fund. I ran the numbers and found that instead of giving each group $7,500 per year they would each receive $7,142 per year. She happily added them.

Ruth's story is a great example of how to use real estate (or appreciated property) to fund a charitable remainder trust, generate income, and receive an income tax deduction. Donating real estate to a charitable remainder trust removes the asset from your estate and can provide an income stream for the rest of your life. The remainder of the proceeds then goes to a directed fund, which distributes an annual grant to one or more charitable organizations.

Personal Reflection

How much money will you give? How many organizations matter? Would you prefer to give smaller grants to more organizations or larger grants to fewer organizations?

_____

_____

_____

_____

_____

CHAPTER 8

DIVORCE

Divorced, No Children

When Sharon Martin came to see me at the Oregon Community Foundation, she was the very first person I worked with at my new job. I greeted her with my warmest smile, but, from the look on her face, I knew something was wrong. Sharon, apparently not one to mince words, shook my hand briskly and said, "I don't have much time for small talk. I don't have much time for anything. My lawyer sent me here because he thinks you'll be able to help me," she added.

Then she said the last thing I expected to hear. "I'm 54 years old, and I've been diagnosed with inoperable ovarian cancer. Wait! Don't say anything. I have to get this out. I've lived a great life. I got out of a bad marriage when I knew it wouldn't work. I built a highly successful career. I've got no kids. I've truly loved almost every minute of my life."

I waited to hear what she would say next. "According to my doctors, I will not be able to beat this disease … in my lifetime. I've got three to five years at best. But, I have money and resources that will be here after I'm gone. Arlene, I'm going to fight this disease from the grave, and you're going to help me."

"I am sorry to hear about your illness, but thank you for wanting to leave the world a better place," I said.

Well, I'm also a no-nonsense kind of woman, so we walked into the conference room and got right down to work. Initially, she considered supporting ovarian cancer research. Maybe she could help them find a cure so other women could survive. Although there are wonderful hospitals in Portland, none specialized in ovarian cancer research. We took our search nationwide and found two top hospitals doing groundbreaking research on ovarian cancer and looking for a cure—the MD Anderson Cancer Center at the University of Texas in Houston and the Fred Hutchinson Cancer Research Center in Seattle, Washington.

After reviewing what both teams were working on, Sharon chose to name the Fred Hutchinson Cancer Research Center in her legacy fund. Her current doctor also worked with them, so she felt comfortable with her choice. She asked me to go ahead and draft a legacy fund that would make her first gift a reality.

I went to her home a week later for our next meeting. She lived in southeast Portland on a peaceful a tree-lined street. The house had a covered porch in the backyard leading to a stunningly beautiful flower garden. She also had a vegetable garden so she could have the freshest vegetables possible, an important part of her health regime.

I handed her the paperwork she'd requested. Sharon began to read the legacy fund agreement and stopped before she finished the first paragraph. It said, "To be used to create a legacy fund, which shall be devoted to the support of the Fred Hutchinson Cancer Research Center for ovarian cancer research." Something just didn't sit right. She wasn't ready to sign it. What's more, she wasn't in the same hurry to get it done as she had been just one week earlier.

"Three to five years seems a lot longer to me than it did the day we met," she said. "I want to let my treatment happen, and I want to see what happens to me and to my life in the process. Let's make a date for one year from today and see where we are."

I went back the following year, and we modified the original document. As it turned out, Sharon outlived her prognosis. I went back to see her each year over the next five years. Each time, we modified the document. On many levels, she had learned to live with the disease. And her priority had shifted from finding a cure for ovarian cancer to helping people with severe illnesses (no matter the disease) stay in their homes as long as possible. How could she give people the quality of life she had been able to provide for herself?

Evolving Values

Working with Sharon reinforced my understanding of philanthropy as a fluid process. Even a person who knows they have a short time to live needs to take the time to think and make informed, heartfelt decisions.

You're not going to just meet someone like me and come away with a plan. Sometimes, you're going to come away with really great ideas that you need to mull over and think about. Philanthropy is for the long haul and not about rushing into a decision. It's about finding a solution that meets your needs and your heart's deepest desire.

Over the years, Sharon and I developed a profound friendship. I continued to check in with her once a year. I'll never forget the last time I went to see her. She was sitting on her back porch, and the sunlight was in her eyes. She could barely breathe. I'd arrived shortly before it was time for her to take her 3:00 p.m. pain pill. Those minutes from 2:50 to 3:03 were the toughest I've ever spent with another living being. Her pain was so severe.

As we sat together, she gripped my hand as the pain surged through her body. Finally, the medication took effect, and she could talk and think clearly. We discussed the Oregon Death with Dignity Act, which allows terminally ill Oregonians to end their lives on their own terms. It was a short conversation. That wasn't the direction she wanted to take.

As the disease had progressed and changed her and her life, Sharon's idea of the kind of legacy she wanted to leave behind had also evolved. Intense personal reflection informed her choice. She shifted from an interest in funding cancer research to knowing that she wanted to support hospice and in-home care for people with terminal illnesses. Hospice provides comfort care along with emotional and spiritual support. Her hospice caregivers were the most thoughtful, kind, and warm individuals she had ever met. She wanted other terminally ill people to have the resources she did at the end of her life. She wanted to help others transition out of this life surrounded by loving care and effective pain management.

Sharon left a profound impact on me. She showed me how to thoughtfully create a legacy. She stayed involved in the process to the very end. Her conversations with her friends, her doctors, her caregivers, and me helped her clarify her philanthropic intentions. It was my honor to work with her and create a means for her to fully realize her goal. Every time I talk to a client who's in that same situation, I think of Sharon and her journey. It gives me the strength to help them make smart choices.

Personal Reflection

You don't need to have a terminal illness to begin thinking about what you want your legacy to be. As you start to think about your legacy and the difference you want to make when you're gone, consider these areas to help you focus more clearly on what is important to you and what you value most:

With this gift, my intention is

___Personal/Spiritual

___Sustaining a cause I love

___Visibility for business or family

___Education

___Arts

___Advocacy and public policy

___Environment

___Other

CHAPTER 9

NEXT GENERATION GIVING

I began working for the Oregon Community Foundation in the summer of 2007. The economy was booming. Many major companies throughout the country were being acquired or merging with larger corporations. Employees with stock options as part of their compensation were becoming wealthy overnight.

Stock Options

During this financial boom, I met Ed and Diane Miller. Ed worked for an international high-tech company, and Diane was a dental hygienist. They were in their late 50s, had two children (ages 6 and 8), and owned their home in Beaverton, Oregon, a suburb of Portland.

Ed was an executive who made a good living. Diane's income was more supplemental. She just loved her work. Over the years, Ed and Diane had worked closely with their financial advisor. They had a sizable nest egg in place. Their advisor helped them start 529 college savings plans for each of their children. The Millers were comfortable, living a good life, and traveling for vacations. They donated to charities through workplace giving campaigns.

They wanted to teach their children about giving back to the community, so they volunteered as a family at the local food bank and helped out at the kids' school. They had causes they cared about and donated money to from time to time, but they had never made a major gift to a charity.

Ed had been with his company for about ten years. During that time, he had received stock options as part of his compensation. When rumors began about a potential merger, Ed and Diane contacted their financial advisor. If the merger went through, it would be a windfall for them, and they wanted to be sure to use this opportunity strategically. One objective was to give to charity. Another was to teach their children about philanthropy. Their financial advisor loved the idea and encouraged them to meet with me for an overview of the charitable giving process.

Our first meeting was an opportunity for us to get to know each other and for me to learn about their values and what was important to them. They had lots of interests—the environment, animals, hiking, biking, and making their own beer. They'd even taken several bike and beer trips through Europe.

Like many people, their giving priorities were still forming. They had areas of interest, but no clear giving pattern. They volunteered every once in a while. Neither of them was currently serving on a nonprofit board.

We discussed some options for their giving:

1) Donate outright to some of the causes they had given to in the past
2) Create a donor-advised fund

The benefit of making outright donations is immediate. You get a tax deduction, and you support an organization(s) you believe in. The cons are that it is a onetime gift and irrevocable. We talked about whether giving this way would provide an example for their children. They didn't think so, and they both wanted more than instant gratification. They wanted an option that involved a long-term commitment to a cause—a relationship that would build over time.

A donor-advised fund seemed to suit these long-term interests. Like an outright donation, a donor-advised fund provides an immediate tax deduction and the ability to support a charity. However, unlike a onetime donation, a donor-advised fund allows for long-term relationships with chosen charities.

The Millers could recommend grants from their fund to support organizations over time.

They could also involve their children in the charitable giving process by designating them to be the fund's advisors when they were no longer able to do it themselves. A donor-advised fund would help them track their giving patterns so they could focus on certain areas or interests. It also would give them unique access to research on different charities. They couldn't find any cons with this option.

Since the Millers wanted to start their fund with stock options, we had to be aware of the restrictions typically associated with stock options. These include knowing the specific limits and/or time frames when you can buy, sell, or transfer stock. Additionally, gifts of stock must be donated prior to when the sale of the company is complete to ensure individuals have true charitable intent. Failure to donate prior to when the sale is complete results in the forfeiture of your charitable tax deduction. This can be tricky, so be sure to work with your advisors on the nuances of these gifts.

Ed and Diane decided to donate $50,000 worth of Ed's company stock to a donor-advised fund at the Oregon Community Foundation (OCF). Two months later, the announcement came that the company would be purchased for $2.8 billion. Upon completion of the sale, their gift instantly appreciated in value, which was another bonus for the Millers. Since then, the Miller family has continued to meet periodically with their donor relationship officer to learn more about charitable giving and what new opportunities the OCF has to offer.

In 2012, the OCF Board of Directors named children's dental health a statewide priority for the foundation. As a dental hygienist, Diane was thrilled. A key project within the initiative was to educate children and families about dental health and to help them learn dental care habits that would protect their teeth and their overall health.

Part of the project was to provide dental health kits throughout the state for kids and families who needed them. Volunteers in every county helped to assemble the kits. In Portland, my daughters and I participated in making them, alongside Diane Miller and her kids, now 11 and 13. It was such a great experience to work with them on this project.

All of the materials were laid out in the OCF conference room. Volunteers then walked down the assembly line with a plastic bag that they filled with a toothbrush, toothpaste, and floss. Diane and I were both overjoyed about the kids' participation. They were engaged, making a difference, and having fun. As a parent, I was inspired watching them work. They helped at each stage of the assembly line and even replaced items on the line as we used them up. I think we made more than 500 bags that day.

As we prepared the kits, one of the OCF staffers educated us on the bleak statistics of dental health in Oregon. Poor dental health led to toothaches that forced kids to miss school. Many of these kids ended up in the emergency room for care, and too many of them had to have teeth extracted far too early in their lives.

Diane and I left the volunteer event with our children feeling fulfilled. She called me the next day to share how pleased she was to participate with the OCF. Dental care was near and dear to her heart and this project was going to make such a difference.

By creating a donor-advised fund, Ed and Diane were able to receive a tax deduction for the donated stock. In addition, it was a great way to lead by example and create a charitable legacy that their children could continue.

Personal Reflection

Who in your life do you want to set an example for about giving back? What would charitable engagement look like with those individuals? What giving areas are near and dear to your heart?

_____

_____

_____

_____

_____

To Inherit or Not To Inherit

Just before you go on vacation, what are some of the chores you do to get ready for your trip? If you're like me (and my family), we get a house sitter to watch the dog, stop the newspaper, make sure the bills are paid, and maybe hire the kid down the block to water the lawn. Well, while Alex and Karen Club were planning their summer of 2012 cross-country motorcycle trip, they happened to get a call from their financial advisor.

They were so excited about the trip they couldn't help sharing how they were going to hike, bike, and fish up and down the west coast for the whole summer. They were retired teachers and used to do these kinds of trips every year. "We've got everything on our checklist done, and we are ready to go!" Karen told her.

"Did reviewing and updating your wills show up on that checklist?" their advisor asked.

"No," said Karen, "we haven't looked at them in years. I think we did those wills when we first got married 10 years ago."

This was a second marriage for both of Alex and Karen. Each had brought an adult son into the marriage. In addition to both of their retirement funds from teaching, Karen had been widowed and also brought a significant inheritance. As a result, their estate was worth a little over $2 million.

When they pulled out the documents, they were shocked. If anything should happen to both of them, they had divided their estate equally between their two sons. That is a plan that should work for most families.

But when Alex and Karen described their boys, Jonathan and Marc, they referred to them as the "good son" and the "other son". It appears the young men had very different values and priorities. Jonathan, the good son, was a medical technician at a physician's practice. When he wasn't working he enjoyed the great outdoors, just like his parents. He volunteered as a mentor with Friends of the Children. According to his parents, everyone adored him. Tragically, Jonathan was killed at the age of 28 in a boating accident.

Marc, the other son, valued material things and lived large. Marc was in advertising and had an image to keep up. He bought a flashy Lexus and spent money like it was water on luxuries and living the high life—often charging up huge balances on his credit cards. Alex and Karen saw him all the time. They loved him, and affectionately referred to him as an MGB, money-grubbing beneficiary. He would come to them asking for a little extra money to make his house payment or to pay off a credit card debt. He also bragged about his high lifestyle.

It was all about him, and he never gave back to the community. They were frustrated that they were never able to instill in him the values of service and giving. The first few times he asked, they gave him money. But, eventually, they stopped. His over-the-top spending habits seemed to keep getting worse, not better.

Because the last estate plan they had drafted divided their assets equally between the boys, Marc would inherit everything. They decided they had to make a change—before they left on vacation.

The attorney who had written their first will had retired, so their financial advisor recommended a few attorneys he thought would be a good fit for them, and she also referred them to me because they wanted to leave some of their money to charitable causes.

They were still interviewing attorneys when they came to see me. They'd apparently lost sleep for several nights. When I asked them what was wrong, the floodgates opened. "If we die, Marc would receive everything," said Karen with tears in her eyes. "He'd squander all we've saved and worked so hard for."

They wanted to do something immediately, in case something should happen to them on that road trip.

So I asked them, "How much does he expect to inherit? What have you prepared him for?"

They told me they had never really discussed any specific amount with Marc. But it was safe to say that he knew they were well off and, with his brother gone, he probably expected to get it all. Alex and Karen's major assets were their retirement accounts.

Here are the options I outlined in that initial meeting:

Specific Bequest

With a specific bequest, the Clubs' will could stipulate who receives what upon their deaths (if they died at the same time). Marc could inherit nothing, or he could inherit a portion of the entire estate but it would be in a lump sum. For example, they could specify $1 million for Marc, and $1 million placed in a directed fund to support the environment.

The thought of Marc getting even half of the money in one lump sum frightened them. They didn't think he had the capacity to handle that much money. This option would not work for them.

Charitable Remainder Trust

The other option we considered was the creation of a charitable remainder trust. Essentially, upon Alex and Karen's deaths, the entire estate of $2 million would be used to create a charitable remainder trust. Marc would receive a yearly income for life and the remainder would go to a directed fund to support the environment after he dies.

If the trust was funded with $2 million and we assumed a 5% payout, Marc would receive an annual distribution of $100,000 per year for the rest of his life. Again, it seemed like too much money to give him, and none of the money would go to the environment until after he died. They nixed that option, too.

"How much do you think is reasonable for him to receive each year?" I asked them.

"$25,000 would be a really nice," they responded.

I worked the calculation backwards. To calculate the size of the trust, you take the annual distribution and multiply it by 20; which gives you $500,000. So a $500,000 trust with a 5% payout would provide $25,000 per year.

This meant they could set up the estate so a $500,000 charitable remainder trust provides Marc with an annual payment of approximately $25,000 dollars. The residual of the estate, $1.5 million, would go to a directed fund to support the environment. When Marc dies, what is left of the charitable remainder trust would go to the directed fund.

This option looked much better, but it still didn't accomplish their goal of instilling the value of service or giving in Marc.

"You can realize all three goals," I told them.

"How?" they asked in unison.

"You can provide an income stream to your son, direct money to the environment, and teach him how to give," I said.

"Well that would be great! What do we have to do?" they asked.

I suggested they set up the estate so that a $500,000 charitable remainder trust would provide Marc with an annual payment of approximately $25,000 dollars. They could then create a donor-advised fund with another $500,000 that would designate Marc as the advisor and give him an opportunity to learn how to give. Finally, the residual of the estate, $1 million, would go to a directed fund to support the environment. When Marc dies, what was left of the charitable remainder trust and the advised fund would transfer to the directed fund.

This was feeling better by the minute. I sent them home to think it through and discuss the options with their new estate-planning attorney.

But, the more they thought about it, the less inclined they were to leave Marc anything. They realized that they'd rather see the results of their life's work and saving strategies go to support the environment they both loved so much.

After meeting with the attorney, they came back to me with a new idea. When I asked what they were going to do, they told me, "Marc is a fun and enjoyable person to hang out with. We love spending time with him. The more we thought about it, the more we realized that our values are very different. We intend to leave him $25,000."

"OK," I said, "You want to set up the charitable trust with $500,000 so he receives about $25,000 per year, right?"

"No. When we met with the attorney, we decided to write Marc out of the will altogether. He is just going to get $25,000, and the rest will go to charity."

They reiterated how he just didn't share their values, and it was important to support what mattered to them. Marc could support himself, but the environment couldn't. "Besides," Alex added, "Marc will do just fine, after he gets over the fact we left him out of the will."

Their decision meant no drafting of a charitable trust. Instead, the will gave a specific bequest of $25,000 to Marc, and the remainder went to a directed fund for environmental organizations of their choosing.

Alex and Karen were elated when they finished creating the funds. They had no intention of telling Marc, because they still wanted to see him at the holidays.

A couple of days later, they were off to enjoy the road on their bikes, fishing and hiking—another pair of self-actualized clients.

Personal Reflection

How much are your children prepared to receive? How much do you think is enough to leave them?

_____

_____

_____

_____

_____

Honoring a Loved One

As the mother of two daughters, both in college at this writing, I can tell you there is nothing that scares me more than the thought of outliving them. I met with Dr. Don Wong and his wife, Kim Chou, to help them create a memorial scholarship for their daughter. Their story put that fear squarely in front of me because they had lived my worst nightmare.

Don and Kim had one daughter, Amy. They adored her. They poured all of their love and devotion into giving her the best that life had to offer. In high school, she was an honor roll student in a challenging International Baccalaureate program as well as an all-star soccer player.

It was an enormous source of joy and pride for them when Amy announced she wanted to follow in her father's footsteps and become a doctor. Just like her father, she received an athletic scholarship to Harvard.

I could easily relate to the bittersweet emotions they felt when they took Amy to get her settled into her dorm at Harvard that sunny September day. They hoped they had equipped her with all the tools and resources she would need to succeed in school and beyond. Her freshman year flew by. Amy adjusted beautifully to student life.

At the end of her first summer vacation, she kissed her parents goodbye and flew off to start her sophomore year. It would be the last time the Wongs held their beloved daughter in their arms. Early in the semester, Amy decided to ride along with a friend into downtown Boston. They were in a terrible accident, and Amy didn't survive.

Kim and Don were devastated. Their one and only child, the beautiful being that was going to carry forward their values, beliefs, and ideals was gone. Through the pain of this tragic loss, they decided to raise money to honor their daughter. They told their friends, family, the young women in Amy's class, and other students and faculty at Harvard. In an outpouring of love and generosity, $20,000 was raised to honor Amy.

The Wongs had also funded a college savings account for Amy. There was still almost $80,000 in the account. They added that to the money people had donated. Then, overwhelmed with grief, they lost momentum.

It would be five years of grief and sorrow before they were ready to do what needed to be done to create a fund that would honor their beloved daughter. I was working at the Oregon Community Foundation, and they wanted my help to make it happen.

Through my own tears, after hearing their story, I asked them to tell me about the values they wanted this fund to embody. Kim talked about her family's passion for education and helping people. Don had spent many years in school learning and training to be a doctor, in part, because of the influence of his father, who was also a doctor. Taking care of people was all he had ever wanted to do. His father was proud that he followed his path, and Don was proud his daughter had wanted to follow the same path.

"How do you want Amy to be remembered?" I asked.

"We want everyone to remember her as the vibrant, brilliant, and talented young woman she was," Kim answered without hesitation as Don nodded in agreement.

"Where would you like to do that?" I asked.

"Harvard!" they answered in unison. Right away, they both agreed that it should be where Amy had lived and thrived before she died. They wanted to create an athletic scholarship, like the one Amy had received. They wanted to encourage high achieving young women, like Amy, at Harvard.

Memorial Scholarships

Now, we had to work out the details. They told me they had put the $100,000 into a trust account in Amy's name at their bank. I asked if they had a trust drafted and if they had applied for a tax identification number. They had not done either of these things. They had simply named it a trust account, and both of them had signing authority. We could work with that.

At this point, we needed to clarify a few issues. The Wongs needed to consider some specifics about the scholarship and its recipients, and then we needed to consider the financial side of making that happen.

Based on their desire to support high-achieving young women attending Harvard, I wanted to ask them some clarifying questions.

- Is it any young woman?
- Where is she from?
- What makes her high achieving?

As they thought through these questions, they began to focus on young women from Oregon who were similar academically or athletically to Amy. Kim explained, "We want to support one young woman as much as we can, all four years of her undergraduate work at Harvard." Of course, the student would have to remain in good standing for the scholarship to recur.

Recurring scholarships are not as common for freshman as one-time scholarships. With the high cost of education, especially at an Ivy League school, it's no surprise that there are many students who cannot continue their education due to lack of money. This scholarship in Amy's name would make a huge difference for one worthy student.

After setting the scholarship's objectives, we were ready to deal with the financial side of things. Kim and Don had set aside this money to honor Amy in an interest bearing savings account at their bank.

What were their options?

1) Transfer the $100,000 from the savings account to the Oregon Community Foundation to create the scholarship. In this scenario, they would receive an immediate tax deduction based on the donation of $100,000.

2) Transfer appreciated securities in the amount of $100,000 to the Oregon Community Foundation. In this scenario, they would receive an immediate tax deduction as a result of the $100,000 gift and avoid capital gains taxes on those securities.

After discussing these possibilities, the Wongs realized that the money in that account had a very specific meaning for them. Despite the better tax options they could get from donating securities, they chose to donate all of the money in the account to the Oregon Community Foundation for the scholarship. Their emotional attachment wasn't to the bank account. It was its meaning as a link to their daughter, and they wanted to see it become a living memory of her. It was important for me to recognize, respect, and honor that emotional attachment.

I next asked them about their estate plans. "Well, we have no other children and our parents are gone," Don answered. "Can we leave all of our assets to the fund?" he asked. Yes, they could. They would need to update certain documents, including (but not limited to) a will and an IRA beneficiary designation form.

After we completed the paperwork to establish the scholarship fund through the Oregon Community Foundation, Kim and Don were actually able to smile. They had kept their promise to use all the donations they'd received to honor Amy. They were proud, tired, and looking forward to providing a young woman with the opportunity to learn and grow in the same academic environment their daughter had so loved.

They were also a little excited because the fund was set up so that they could select the scholarship recipient. They were moving forward and ensuring that the Amy Wong Memorial Scholarship Fund made a difference in one deserving young woman's life.

The impact of this gift would create a ripple of positive effects—starting in Oregon, moving across the country to Harvard, and then beyond to the world. After Don and Kim passed, more money would go into the fund, and more students would benefit from their generous gift. The solution we created for them incorporated giving during their lives and giving through their estate plan through a bequest and beneficiary designations.

This story is an example of how a tragedy was turned around and used to create an amazing opportunity for a young woman just like Amy.

Personal Reflection

Identify two or three people (they could be family members, other people you know, or historic figures) who have been strong influences on you. What values did they transmit to you? What are the values not transmitted that you want to pass down?

_____

_____

_____

_____

_____

CHAPTER 10

MULTIGENERATIONAL GIVING

Marco Romano was the son of Italian immigrants. Growing up, his family had very little money, and everyone worked hard for everything they needed. Marco began working as a teenager and worked his way through college and dental school. He married his high school sweetheart, Maria. Together, they raised four children, two boys and two girls, while building a thriving dental practice.

Marco was also an astute businessman and hired a great money manager. By the time he had retired in 2008, he and his wife were worth $20 million. They were living the American dream. Their children were happily married, and they now had eight grandchildren. They especially loved to celebrate any worthy occasion and hosted most of the family's holiday parties. This meant that they would have up to 40 guests gathered around their table—many times a year.

I met Marco and Maria for the first time in 2014. Both their attorney and accountant referred them to me. I visited with them at their lovely home just outside of Portland, Oregon. The house was atop a mountain. I drove up a winding road shaded by hundreds of trees. The view from the top took my breath away. The outside of their home had a clean and simple design. When I walked through the front door, the picture window in the entryway opened to a stunning view of Oregon wine country.

As they led me through the house to the family room, I was privileged to see their amazing art collection, paintings, sculptures, and a different view of the valley from each room. Empty nesters, they shared their home with two friendly and well-behaved French bulldogs who escorted us every step of the way.

From the moment I met Marco, I could see why he was so successful. Our discussion started with him telling me how he'd worked his entire adult life. By the time he had retired, he had already put all four of the children through college and given his wife a very good life. When Marco first started the practice, Maria had helped by doing the bookkeeping. After their first son was born, she'd take him with her to work. A couple of years later, after their first daughter was born, they were doing well enough for Maria to stay at home to raise them. She volunteered on the school's PTA, and all the children's friends were welcome in their home after school and on weekends. She was everyone's mom.

One thing that set Marco apart from many small business owners I meet is that he recognized the value of surrounding himself with good advisors. Those advisors had helped him make some lucrative financial decisions. As a result, in addition to being able to take care of his immediate family, Marco happily provided college educations for his five nieces and seven nephews. He had also set up trust funds for each of his children. Additionally, all eight grandchildren had 529 college saving plans in place that were funded by Marco and Maria.

It appeared that they literally had everything they could ever want. I asked them, "How can I help you?"

Marco answered, "We've given our kids this rich life. They haven't wanted for anything that money could buy." He took Maria's hand in his and added, "What makes our life so much richer has been our ability to give back and make a difference over the years."

"We want our children to continue that tradition," Maria chimed in, "and we want our grandchildren to carry that tradition forward as well. How do we do that, Arlene? How do we make that happen?"

Before I could give them that answer, I wanted to know more about what was important to them. What were their other passions and interests? Marco loved being a dentist. Even though he had retired, he continued to volunteer with the Tooth Taxi, a state nonprofit that provides dental services throughout rural Oregon. He also volunteered to help people without access to dental care in Africa. He shared that he was so grateful for the opportunities his amazing career had given him and his family that he'd endowed a chair at the dental school. He felt as if he'd given dentistry as much as he could and now wanted to make a difference in other areas.

So, I asked, "What else is important to you?"

Immediately Marco responded that animals and the environment were important to him. When I asked why, he said, "For more than 30 years, I've traveled overseas to help with people's dental issues. On these trips, I couldn't help but notice the heartbreaking abuse and neglect of animals in so many of the places I visited. Just as bad was seeing the environment being pillaged and animal habitats being destroyed." He took Maria's hand in his again and added, "We cannot sustain ourselves if the environment and animals are no longer with us." She nodded in agreement.

I shared with them that only three percent of all giving goes to animals and the environment. They were shocked. This fact and their deep desire to make a difference in this area solidified their decision to create a fund.

Leading the Next Generation

Marco also reflected on the importance of taking care of the most vulnerable. I acknowledged what a beautiful thing it would be to share this passion and pass down a tradition of giving back in their family. "Yes!" he replied. "Our family, our children, and grandchildren are all taken care of. Now, we want to know what we can do with the kind of money we have."

It was clear to me that, because of their considerable resources and strong desire to protect animals and the environment, they had many options. But, this was their money and their passion. I wanted to guide the conversation to specific ways they could engage their children and grandchildren in the giving process.

Several of their grandchildren were just three- or four-year-olds. Even at that young age, children can learn the values of good work and gratitude.

1) Lead by example—Marco accomplished this through his volunteer dental work around the world.
2) Give meaningful books as gifts, such as:
   a. The Giving Tree, by Shel Silverstein
   b. The Lorax, by Dr. Seuss
   c. The Mitten Tree, by Candice Christianse

For school-aged children who are seven to 12 years old, I recommended:

1) Family projects and volunteering
2) Family rituals
3) Developing their own charitable donations

For teenagers, I suggested:

1) Participating in community service or social activism projects
2) Working on e-philanthropy
3) Encouraging brand-conscious purchases that give back, including:
   a. Warby Parker (eyewear)
   b. TOMS (shoes)
   c. Better World Books
   d. Bombas (socks)

And for everyone, I suggested using family gatherings throughout the year to share the stories of giving and making a difference. Marco and Maria were excited about the many possible options and how they could be used to engage their grandchildren in the giving process.

Family Engagement

Our next step was to discuss the details of how this was going to work. For simplicity, I suggested that they create two donor-advised funds—one for supporting the environment and animals, and the other for family giving. They nodded their agreement.

"The first fund is for just you two," I said. "You can support all the animal and environmental organizations you want. The other fund is a donor-advised fund that is generational. This is the one we will use to engage your family."

"Wow, this sounds great. But, with such a big family and so many competing interests, how do we engage each family member? How do we get the others to support the whole process?" Marco asked.

I used the numbers to show them how this could work. If you create a donor-advised fund today, and you put in, say $120,000, then you can make the fund wholly expendable. That means you and your family can grant $120,000 to as many or as few nonprofits as you choose. In my experience with my own family and the many families I work with, doing this together brings families closer together. It's one of the reasons I love what I do.

For this example, I used round numbers, so it's easy to understand. I chose $120,000 because there were 12 family members. You can use any amount you choose.

In my experience, there are two ways to engage a family—individually and collectively. I suggested to Marco and Maria that they do a little bit of both. For individual giving, I recommended they give each person in the family a specific amount that that person could then give to a nonprofit organization of their choice. That way, each individual gives to a cause they care about. Marco and Maria smiled as they nodded their heads in agreement. So, let's take $60,000 and let each family member have $5,000 to give away as they wished. That would be engaging, right? Right.

With the remaining $60,000, Marco and Maria decided the family would choose one or two organizations to support with a major gift—the entire $60,000 or two gifts of $30,000. It's a strategic way to give, and the amount is significant enough to make an impact. They were intrigued and eager to get started. These options matched their resources, their interests, and their family dynamics. It seemed like the perfect solution.

Marco and Maria decided to introduce their plans at their next Thanksgiving dinner. They knew everyone would be there. Each member of the family would get a certain dollar amount to give away. Then, at Christmas, they would come back and share what organization they had given the gift to and why.

To start, Marco and Maria would be the advisors on the family donor-advised fund. When they died, their children (Matteo, Gabriela, Leo, and Rosa) would become the main advisors, and so on with the grandchildren. Also, when Marco and Maria passed away, $10 million dollars would go into the fund for the family to grant into the community.

They created the donor-advised fund with $120,000. The paperwork was standard; however, as the donors, they had a few additional options to choose from.

1) They could name additional successor advisors. Please note: This depends on the sponsoring organization. Not all donor-advised funds allow the option of successor advisors.

2) They had a choice about whether the donor-advised fund was to be wholly expendable or endowed with a payout policy that varies by organization.

After setting up their fund, the Romanos received the full tax deduction allowable by the IRS for the $120,000 donation.

When Grandma Maria announced the plan at Thanksgiving, everyone raised a glass of wine to celebrate the wonderful gift. They were all excited by the possibilities of giving to causes they loved. By the time they got together at Christmas to talk about their giving, the energy around the table was amazing.

Everyone wanted to be the first to share their giving story. They decided to go in age order, with three-year-old Georgia, the youngest, going first. She chose to give at her day school for kids who don't have school lunch. Her grandparents' eyes were glistening with tears of pride and gratitude. Then, one after another, each child in the family shared where they had given and why. It was so much fun. Later, Marco told me that this was the best Christmas ever.

Can you imagine a Christmas where instead of having it be about opening gifts that you don't even need, you talk about the difference you have made in the world. That's what happened to this family. Now, it's an annual tradition, and it **did** bring them closer together.

I know that most of us want to honor our fathers, grandfathers, mothers, and grandmothers. We also want to make a difference. This family set up a way for their children to continue to walk the walk of giving back. It was my honor to help them create it.

One more thing: you don't need to be a millionaire to give this way.

Personal Reflection

Like anything else, giving takes planning. Consider your circumstances, and what makes sense for you. How much will you give? Will it be an annual, a multi-year, or an end-of-life gift? How can you involve your family in the giving process?

_____

_____

_____

_____

_____

_____

_____

_____

Changing Generations, Changing Values

Like many people, I've wished for a wealthy maiden aunt or bachelor uncle who would leave all their money to my cousins and me. No such luck in my family. But, the Wagner family had Great Aunt Sally.

The day I met her, an anguished Sally Wagner arrived at my office early in the morning. She was the matriarch of her family, and the sole trustee of the family foundation her father had created more than 50 years ago. She was deeply concerned because most members of her family had stopped participating in the annual grantmaking process. Those who did participate in the work of the foundation lacked any enthusiasm. She was beginning to prepare for the next annual meeting, just a few months away, and was at a complete loss about what to do. Her attorney had sent her to speak with me.

"I'm here to help you, Sally, what is going on?" I said as I walked this lovely, distinguished 85-year-old woman into our conference room.

Sally's father had made his fortune in the timber business. Her dad would be considered a self-made millionaire, but he never forgot that he couldn't have accomplished all that he had without the hard work of his employees. He wanted to show them how grateful he was, so he set up a private foundation to support local charities in their close-knit community.

Those annual grants made an immense difference to many people in that community. Sally was proud of her role carrying on the tradition of giving and helping that her father had begun. The foundation was her passion. She realized that if she didn't act now, she might not be able to pass these family values of giving to the younger generation. She wanted the next generation of her family to keep the foundation's commitment to the excellent work it funded. When we met, the assets in the foundation were $3 million.

Sally was the youngest of five brothers and sisters. She is now the last of her generation. With her parents and siblings gone, Sally inherited millions. She never married or had children of her own, but her sisters and brothers did. As a result, Sally's heirs are her eight nieces and nephews as well as 12 great-nieces and great-nephews. Family members range in age from 10 to 85 years old.

Until now, Sally has managed the foundation mostly on her own, with family members attending a yearly meeting. However, she wants to figure out how to engage them in the work of the foundation. She isn't sure where to begin, and that's where I can help.

This year, Sally is especially excited because the foundation will be able to grant $150,000, which is equal to five percent of the foundation's corpus and the amount the IRS requires private foundations to give in order to keep their nonprofit status. But, she isn't sure whether her nieces and nephews and their children even care.

"When you talked with them, what did they say?" I asked.

She had a blank look on her face and then smiled, "I've never really asked them to do anything but attend the meeting and listen to me talk about all the grants we were going to make together ... maybe I should rethink my approach," she said, her face lighting up with a winning smile.

I helped her think through what she wanted to learn from her family. We settled on three simple open-ended questions. The plan was for her to call each relative to speak with them privately. She would ask:

1) What is working?
2) What is not working?
3) What ideas and suggestions do you have?

Sally's first call was to one of her nieces who responded, "We feel that this giving has always been for you and your generation. When we come to a meeting, it seems like you just want us to rubberstamp what you've decided. There is nothing for us to do or say. You don't seem to want our input." Her niece's feedback was eye-opening for Sally. She wasn't sure what she would hear from the rest of her nieces and nephews, but she was committed to figuring out how to get the next generation involved in the family foundation, so she kept calling.

One of her nephews and two of her grandnephews had moved out of the area. They lived in Georgia, Hawaii, and Maine. While she knew they led busy lives and that it was a long distance to travel, she never quite understood why they couldn't make this one foundation meeting per year a priority. After all, Oregon was their home. But, Sally's out-of-state family felt differently. Almost like an echo, they explained, "Except for you, Aunt Sally, we don't really have a connection to Oregon. We love you, but we'd rather give closer to our real homes."

The biggest shock came when she called one of her nephews in Oregon, and his wife answered. He was out for the day, but, after Sally explained why she was calling, she was told, "Aunt Sally, I don't think anyone else in the family will tell you this, but I am going to take a leap here. The only reason any of us show up for that meeting and go along with your grantmaking choices is because we're afraid you'll disinherit us if we don't." This was a tough thing to hear.

Sally was saddened and discouraged when she shared the results of the calls with me. She couldn't think of a way to engage her family in a way that would be relevant to them and wondered if it was even possible to get them to care as much about the foundation as she did. She was ready to do something dramatic to capture their attention.

I had a big grin on my face as I said, "Sally, this is great news. Thanks to your calls, we have enough information to create a plan that I think you will really like."

Here are some of the options I suggested Sally consider:

1) Continue current grantmaking to the local community
2) Restructure grant distributions
3) Dissolve or spend down the private foundation
4) Do nothing

Sally paused and reflected on these options. Doing nothing was not her style. She loved the idea of still supporting her dad's local charities, but, just as importantly, she wanted to engage the family. Instead of making a decision that day, she decided to go back and discuss the different giving options with her family. I knew she was on the right track.

It was no surprise to me that the family was thrilled to be invited to participate in the process of choosing new ways to give. Sally was delighted that they were, too. She hadn't expected that to happen. After much discussion, they decided as a family that these were the best four options:

1) Give each family a portion of the annual distribution to direct to a charity of their choice

2) Collaborate with the entire family to make one large donation

3) Allow grants to be made closer to their homes

4) Do a combination of the above options

Sally and I reviewed the pros and cons of each option. She loved the idea of giving locally and could appreciate the family wanting to give in their hometowns. She decided to give each family $20,000 to give to a charity of their choice. Between that day and the next big holiday gathering, they would do their research and share with the others information about the causes they wanted to support.

When they arrived for that family gathering, there was more energy and excitement than Sally had ever seen. Family members had brought ideas and information about their charities. They were excited to share pamphlets with details about different charities, and one younger family member even created an online presentation using Prezi. One family made two significant grants, while another decided to make 30 smaller awards that mirrored awards that Grandpa had given. Everyone had found a new sense of caring, compassion, and commitment to giving. The next generation had found a new way to carry on the family legacy of giving started by Sally's dad.

Over the years, the family maintained this new vigor with the foundation. They continued to engage in thoughtful conversations about their philanthropy. After Sally passed, they all agreed that the foundation would be divided into four separate donor-advised funds—one fund for family in each state: Oregon, Maine, Georgia and Hawaii. This is a good example of how a private foundation can be dissolved into a donor-advised fund(s).

By opening the discussion and identifying ways to make giving relevant, Sally succeeded beyond her expectations in engaging the next generation. Best of all, the end result made everyone happy. The family learned that their Aunt Sally loved them dearly, and she made sure to let them all know they would receive a gift as her bequest to them.

Personal Reflection

Where have you spent your time and money in the past? Why? Are these activities and organizations still meaningful to you? If not, what changes would you make? Where do you want to spend your time and money now?

_____

_____

_____

_____

_____

CHAPTER 11

HOW TO CHOOSE AND WORK WITH AN ADVISOR

Choosing the Right Advisor for You

As you can see from each story in this book, a team of experts were instrumental in advising givers. When you bring together your professional team, you can accomplish charitable giving in ways you never imagined possible. Your team may include the following individuals: financial advisor, accountant, attorney, banker, trust officer, insurance agent and brokers and fundraising professionals. There are a lot of moving parts to consider when pulling together your team, which makes it critical for you to select advisors you know, like, and trust.

Here are some questions to think about when choosing an advisor:

- How did you learn about this advisor?
- How well do you know them?
- Do they have a digital presence?
- What is their focus?
- Do they participate in the community?

- Who referred them to you? What was their experience when they worked with them?

- Do you like them?

- Are they like-minded—are their values a match with yours?

- Do you trust them?

- What degrees and certifications do they hold? Credentials matter.

- Are they members of professional organizations?

- Does the advisor follow a fiduciary standard? Fiduciary standards have your best interest at heart.

If you do not have an advisor, consider interviewing a number of them until you find someone you like and trust. Advisors are there to help during both the good and the bad times, so you need to feel comfortable with them. You want a person who understands you and who can educate and guide you as you plan for the future. Hopefully, that future will include a legacy giving plan that means something to you and allows you to make a positive difference.

During the selection process, you'll want to determine the type of advice or services you'll need.

- Investment

- Taxes

- Estate law

- Estate planning

- Insurance

- Retirement planning

- Charitable giving

- Trust creation

- Trust administration and management

- Fiduciary

If you are comfortable, ask for referrals. Referrals can even come from another advisor. For example, your accountant may have worked with well-qualified estate planning attorneys. Your financial planner may have a colleague in the insurance field. Family and friends are also good sources for referrals.

From these various sources, create a list of possible advisors and then do your research. This is essential. Find out what you can about the person you're considering to entrust with your financial future. Check out their digital presence. What is their website like? What do their LinkedIn and/or Facebook profiles look like? Depending on the type of advisor you're seeking, look into the types of certifications they have and their membership in professional organizations.

Once you've narrowed the field, pick the three that resonate most with you. Reach out to each of them for a one-on-one meeting so you can interview them and decide if this is someone who would work well with you.

During the interview, ask questions—lots of questions. Before you begin a formal relationship, you want to find out about this professional's areas of expertise, and what fees are associated with specific tasks. If you have significant assets, don't be hasty. Consider the amount of money you will be investing or donating. Remember that good advice is worth it. Bad advice, at any price, is too costly.

For example, let me explain how important your estate-planning attorney can be for you, your heirs, and/or your beneficiaries. Imagine you are having chest pain. You call 911. The EMTs arrive and take you straight to the emergency room. As they wheel you in, you need to think about who you want taking care of you ... your family physician, your dermatologist, or a cardiovascular surgeon? The answer is—you want a specialist. The same is true with your financial team. Yes, estate planning can be that precise.

When choosing a fiduciary to act on your behalf to manage your assets as part of a trust, you'll want to meet with them before you finalize your trust documents. This way, you and you representative can be clear about your objectives, values, and instructions.

How to Prepare To Meet With Your Advisor

Estate planning can either be fairly simple and straight-forward or highly complex—depending on your net worth, the kinds of assets you own, and the number of heirs and other beneficiaries you have. The more you know about estate planning and your options, the easier it will be to take care of your loved ones and incorporate into your plan a charitable gift you might never have imagined possible.

Regardless of how much you know or don't know, there are advisors who can help you. Whether you are just starting out with a little nest egg or are a highly sophisticated investor, an effective advisor can help people at every knowledge and investment level.

Before you meet with an advisor, here's list of the financial information you'll need to have available:

Financial Information Needed

- List of your assets and liabilities
- Current income and projected future income
- Annual or monthly budget—current and future needs
- Projected nonrecurring expenses—major house repair or project
- Number of dependents you are responsible for
- Health or external issues personally or in your family
- Current financial statements for your IRA(s) and 401(k)s, and any other funds or investment accounts
- Social Security benefits for you and your spouse or a disabled family member
- A copy of your latest tax return (personal and business)

Other Information Needed

- Wills that may be in force
- Trusts you have created or are the beneficiary of
- IRA and 401(k) beneficiary designations
- Pension beneficiary designations
- Insurance designations
- Records of your defined benefits, deferred compensation, or other employee benefits
- Power of Attorney
- Deeds to all real property you own or hold a mortgage on

Tips for Talking With Your Advisor

Remember this chart from chapter 1? You should be able to easily engage with your advisor in all areas of your life. That is why it is so important that you take your time to select an advisor who meets your needs. When times are difficult, it will be important that you're able to provide your advisor with details about what is happening, including obstacles or challenges. Without all of this information, it's tough for them to create a comprehensive plan.

Comprehensive/Holistic Planning

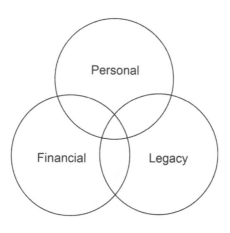

When you share personal information, talk about any inheritance a family member has received or may be in line to receive. Let them know if there are difficult relationships or people who might dispute or fight any of your choices. Talk about any of your loved ones who may need ongoing care or financial support. Think about how much money your heirs are prepared to receive and in what form they should receive it.

When discussing your financial goals, talk about any tax concerns, the succession plan you have (or don't have) for your business, and any assets you might want or need to sell. Whether you know your investment risk tolerance or not, share your situation as fully as you can.

Be sure to include your legacy goals, even if aspirational. Take some time to review your personal reflections throughout this book, and start to think about how you want to be remembered as you begin your philanthropic journey.

You and your advisors should align. It should feel good that someone understands and can articulate back your complete objectives, and, in the process of having these dialogues, you may even uncover your legacy.

An ideal financial plan helps you find your generous side, helps you engage your community, helps you feel good about helping others, and, ultimately, helps you make a difference. Imagine making a leadership gift to a cause near and dear to your heart. Imagine seeing the changes you can make as a family when you come together to make a difference. You can change the world through your leadership and philanthropy, and you will be happier.

Go out and buy your stairway to heaven, because money can buy you happiness if you give to causes you care about.

TESTIMONIALS

Our team has always appreciated your professional expertise in helping us help our clients to connect the most effective strategies and tools with their heartfelt support of what matters to them.

Patrick J Green, Partner,
Davis Wright Tremaine, LLP

Arlene Siegel Cogen is a true professional. Her infectious personality and deep knowledge of charitable gift planning make her an absolute pleasure to work with. Ever since I arrived in Portland eight years ago she has been a wonderful resource, advocate and friend.

Marc Blattner, CEO of Jewish Federation
of Greater Portland

I had the pleasure of working with Arlene for several years when she was with The Oregon Community Foundation, and she clearly "gets" the world of philanthropy.

Jeffrey C. Thede, Partner, Thede, Culpepper,
Moore, Monroe & Silliman, LLP

I have had the privilege of knowing Arlene for many years. I find her to be warm, compassionate, and fun, with a no nonsense personality. She is knowledgeable in her field of expertise and is a thoughtful, strategic thinker. It has been my pleasure to have her coach my colleagues as well as introduce her to my clients. I will look forward to working with Arlene throughout the years to come.

Michelle Castano Garcia, Principal,
Northwest Investment Counselors

I have known Arlene as a congregant and consultant for the past 4 years. As a campaign professional she has helped galvanize, energize and educate our core of solicitors. She is professional, kind and supportive.

Eve Posen, Assistant Rabbi,
Congregation Neveh Shalom

ABOUT THE AUTHOR

Arlene Cogen, CFP

Arlene Cogen is an experienced philanthropic leadership consultant who works closely with professional advisors, nonprofits, and their clients to foster deep relationships, engage the next generation, and make a lasting difference through leadership and philanthropy.

A Certified Financial Planner (CFP), Arlene spent over 20 years in the trust and investment world on the leadership teams of numerous major financial institutions. Desiring change and the opportunity to give back, Arlene acquired nonprofit development expertise and excellence by helping to guide the ninth largest community foundation in the country for almost a decade.

Arlene was the first nonprofit leader to hold a board position on the Portland Estate Planning Council. Arlene's other professional affiliations include the Financial Planning Association, National Speakers Association, Northwest Planned Giving Roundtable, and the Oregon Philanthropic Advisors Network.

When you work with Arlene, you get an expert perspective on giving derived from her broad experiences with individuals and businesses ranging from Wall Street to Main Street.

ArleneCogen.com
Arlene@ArleneCogen.com
503-957-8334

THANK YOU

When I walk into a sacred space, I say the Shehecheyanu. The Shehecheyanu blessing is said on special occasions and when thankful for new and unusual experiences. For me, writing this book was a sacred duty, and the completion was the ultimate special occasion.

בָּרוּךְ אַתָּה יְיָ אֱלֹהֵינוּ מֶלֶךְ הָעוֹלָם, שֶׁהֶחֱיָנוּ וְקִיְּמָנוּ וְהִגִּיעָנוּ לַזְּמַן הַזֶּה.

Baruch atah Adonai, Eloheinu Melech haolam, shehecheyanu, v'kiy'manu, v'higianu laz'man hazeh

Our praise to You, Eternal our God, Sovereign of all: for giving us life, sustaining us, and enabling us to reach this season.

If you found this book valuable, make an appointment with your advisors to discuss your legacy and begin your philanthropic journey.

Follow me on social Media.

LinkedIn: https://www.linkedin.com/in/arlenecogen/
Twitter: @ArleneCogen

Have FUN doing the most good.

Arlene

Arlene@arlenecogen.com
ArleneCogen.com